Multisensory Environments

Paul Pagliano

David Fulton Publishers
London

David Fulton Publishers Ltd
Ormond House, 26–27 Boswell Street, London WC1N 3JD

First published in Great Britain by David Fulton Publishers 1999

Note: The right of Paul Pagliano to be identified as the author of this work has been asserted by him in accordance with the Copyright, Designs and Patents Act 1988.

British Library Cataloguing in Publication Data
A catalogue record for this book is available from the British Library

ISBN 1–85346–553–4

Typeset by Saxon Graphics Ltd, Derby
Printed in Great Britain by The Cromwell Press Ltd, Trowbridge, Wilts.

Dedication

To my dear wife Fiona whose ongoing support made this book possible, my sons Zachary, Christopher and Matthew and my parents Muriel and Joseph.

Contents

Acknowledgements

I would like to thank the staff and students of Mundingburra Special School for inviting me to be a part of their Multisensory Environment. In particular I would like to thank the principal Bryan Hughes and his secretary Gail Brodie for their assistance. Research conducted at Mundingburra Special School was made possible by two School Based Research Grants funded by the Northern Region of the Queensland Department of Education. James Cook University funded my six months special study leave which provided me with the space to write this book.

Thanks to Dr Heather Mason, Senior Lecturer, School of Education, University of Birmingham for her hospitality during my sabbatical. Heather opened doors for me. Thanks also to staff at the University of Birmingham, particularly Professor Harry Daniels for writing the Foreword, Mike McLinden for ongoing support with literature, and Claire Marvin, Heather Murdoch, Drs Lani Florian, Penny Lacey, Jill Porter and Christina Tilstone for their valuable discussions.

I am especially grateful to Richard Rose, Senior Lecturer in Special Education, Nene College of Higher Education and Dr Barbara Watson, Lecturer in Special Education, James Cook University for being my critical friends. Richard and Barbara both read my book from beginning to end and made many valuable comments and suggestions. Richard helped me feel comfortable that the book made sense across national borders. Barbara helped me feel comfortable that the book was consistent theoretically. Thanks also David Fulton for taking on this project.

Finally, I would like to acknowledge the very extensive support I received from my wife, Dr Fiona McWhinnie. She has proof read and criticised every draft of this book and has spent many hours working behind the scenes attending to details and ensuring that the book was the best I could possibly make it. Without her support and guidance I would not have been able to write it.

Foreword

This volume is a very welcome addition to the literature on the use of multisensory environments (MSE) in the education of children with multiple disabilities. As Paul Pagliano suggests in his title for Chapter 1 'What is a multisensory environment?' the very term MSE has been used to cover a very wide range of arrangements. This broad range of interventions has had a widespread international uptake in special schools over the past ten years. Their educational value remains, to some extent, obscured beneath the very enthusiasm with which their sales have been promoted. It would be too easy to dismiss this phenomena as an example of the lure of technology.

Far too much of the educational practice still proceeds on the basis of relative ignorance of the outcomes of specific interventions. The development of evidence-based practice in education requires us all to bring much more systematic evaluation and reflection to our work. This is not to suggest that clinical evaluation and reflection through, for example, the randomised controlled trials so familiar in medicine is sufficient. We need to know how systems such as MSEs can work as well as how they are used and how their use can be improved *in situ*. This represents a significant challenge. It is clear that children with complex needs present complex teaching problems to all those who work with them in schools. As David Wood reminds us, the everyday business of teaching is more complicated than many would have us believe:

> Monitoring children's activity, remembering what one had said or done to prompt that activity and responding quickly to their efforts at an appropriate level is a demanding intellectual feat. Effective teaching is as difficult as the learning it seeks to promote. (Wood 1991)

Understanding how new technologies enter into the world of the classroom and how they are interpreted and used by teachers and children requires careful thought and systematic observation. A comprehensive critical appraisal has been long overdue. This book is an invitation to professionals working with MSEs to reconsider what educational purposes they may be used to fulfil. Although it is practical, this is not a cookbook. Rather it is ultimately a considered evaluation of the strengths and limitations of the MSE. If educators (i.e. the whole transdisciplinary team – occupational therapist, physiotherapist, speech therapist, teacher, parents) are intelligent, sensitive, and work in collaboration with each other, the MSE can provide a rich vein of opportunity to design learning environments that match the learning needs, interests and abilities of each individual child.

Above all, we need to ensure that technology can help children with multiple disabilities to become active learners, rather than passive recipients of knowledge. Systems of education for all should be as diverse as the needs of the community of learners they seek to serve. Understanding and responding to complex needs requires creative, diligent and proficient teaching. MSEs can be used as powerful tools which provide new means of mediation between teacher and learner. The introduction of technology into an instructional context can transform the dynamics and patterns of the communication system as well as create possibilities for participation and thus for pathways to understanding. It also has the potential to act as a non-educational device for filling time and rendering passive those whose way of thinking and learning interrupts the flow of classrooms in which concern is more with 'getting through' or even entertaining rather than educating.

In order to make best use of these tools we need to understand their potential strengths as well as their limitations. This book helps us to understand more about these important devices and points the way forward to the development of reflective and appropriately critical educational practice. It is indeed a very welcome text.

Harry Daniels
Birmingham
August 1998

Preface

My goal throughout this text has been to avoid bias in language when considering how MSEs can materially assist those with disabilities. In language which refers to disability, I state the person first and the descriptor second. There are exceptions, such as the use of the term 'Deaf'. This is because many deaf individuals state they prefer to be referred to as such. On occasions I also use the term 'Blind' for similar reasons. To avoid gender bias both male and female pronouns are included whenever a singular pronoun is used. In quotations where either the male or female pronoun has been omitted, the missing pronoun has been added in square brackets.

A problem was encountered when choosing disability terminology, particularly because different terms are used in the UK, USA and Australasia for broadly similar concepts, but each with subtle differences and connotations. Originally I adopted the British terminology and tried to use it consistently throughout. For example the term 'learning difficulties' is used to describe any disability-related difficulties with learning. However on occasions I felt that a non-British term would be more appropriate to the context. In Australian Sign Language (ASL) there is acceptance of multiple signs ('sign synonymy and polysemy are accepted and encouraged') to express the same basic idea but with different nuances (Parker *et al.*, 1996, p.v.). As I wrote the book I began to feel that it should be possible to use multiple terminology to describe disability. The reader who has been brought up on a diet of single terms may initially find it disruptive. I hope this initial disruption will give way to acceptance and a richer understanding.

The word 'educator' is used throughout as an inclusive term to refer to all members of the transdisciplinary team working on an individual education programme where the common focus is the child's educational development. The term 'educator' can therefore refer to parents, communication therapists, occupational therapists, physiotherapists as well as teachers and teachers' aides.

I do not use the word 'training' (apart from when the term appears in quotations) because of:

1. *the negative historical association.* Prior to the 1975 US Senate enactment of PL94–142, individuals with intellectual impairment were generally

deemed to be either educable or trainable. The implication was that those with severe or profound intellectual disability were unable to be educated and therefore outside the remit of education.

2. *the negative teaching strategy association.* Training implies that an individual's behaviour is being directed by someone with the explicit aim to achieve a predetermined and habit-like response. Mithaug *et al.* (1988) claimed that inappropriate teaching strategies, particularly in the 'training' direction, encourage dependence and passivity in the student. Dependency and passivity are clearly behaviours which ill serve individuals with disabilities in later life.

> Special education teachers and others using this approach are in charge. They control the entire teaching–learning environment, from setting classroom and student expectations for performance and determining what tasks the student will perform, to the allocation of time for each task, prescribing how it is to be performed, correcting work, providing immediate feedback, and then directing the student to the next step in the curriculum . . . Teacher roles are independent and action oriented, requiring choices, decisions, and self-initiated work. Student roles are dependent and passive, requiring compliance to directives and responses to teacher cues and consequences. Teacher roles are 'adult-like', while students' are 'child-like'. Adults make decisions, plan their work, and take responsibility for seeing that important tasks get done and is correct. Teachers are adults and students are children, right? (pp. 27–28)

Autonomy improves students' entry into adult life. Actively giving students the freedom to be autonomous is the antithesis of 'training'. The goal is equity of freedom for all students.

3. *the negative association with MSE use.* There is a danger that the educator, when using the MSE with children with learning difficulties, will take control in ways that seek to achieve predetermined, habit-like responses. This approach is as inappropriate as the opposite extreme, where the child is simply placed in the MSE and ignored. The educator must be able to use professional insight to design a programme for the MSE that promotes autonomy but with sufficient educator presence to ensure that the child is constantly challenged to achieve his or her highest potential.

4. *the negative association with MSE educator preparation.* Rather than being 'trained' to teach in prescribed ways, MSE educators must learn to think for themselves, become professionally competent, responsible and accountable, so that they are capable of making informed decisions based on knowledge of the individual child, the research literature (regarding the child, disability and the MSE), as well as be able to work collaboratively with a transdisciplinary team (see Chapter 5).

Overview

This book is written in four parts. Part I 'Foundations' consists of Chapters 1, 2 and 3. Chapter 1 'What is a multisensory environment?' provides a general introduction to the field. The MSE can be different things to different people. It can describe an actual space, or the impact that space has on an individual. Furthermore it can be for adults or children, for recreation, leisure, therapy or education. In Chapter 2 'Survey of the MSE literature', MSE uses identified in the literature are sorted into two distinct classifications, namely 'single-minded' and 'open-minded' spaces. Single-minded MSEs describe a space which fulfils a single function whereas open-minded MSEs describe a multi-functional space where uses change depending upon user and need. Chapter 3 'Developing a theoretical perspective of the MSE' examines research literature outside the MSE to identify information that could reasonably be used to inform open minded MSE use (sensorimotor, play, Nielsen, Ayres and O'Brien).

Part II 'Design and construction' explores the what, who, why and how of the open-minded MSE. Chapter 4 'What facilities could be included in the MSE?' lists eight types of MSE (white room, dark room, sound room, inter-active room, water room, soft play room, verandah or garden area) and high-lights a wide range of items that could be incorporated into an open-minded MSE design. In Chapter 5 'Who will be involved in the MSE?', it is argued that an open-minded MSE is best designed through ongoing transdisciplinary collaboration involving all relevant stakeholders: the individual with a disability, parents, carers, educators (teacher, teacher's aide), therapists (occu-pational, physio, communication) and experts in industrial design. This necessitates that the design be flexible, ongoing and constantly able to be adjusted to meet the changing needs of individual users over time. Chapter 6 'Why focus on MSE design and construction?' identifies important reasons behind MSE design and construction as: to enable the individual to develop a concept of 'who am I?', to engineer the environment to match the user's inter-ests, ability, learning style and age, and to promote self-determination, quality of life and social justice. In Chapter 7 'How to design and construct a MSE', issues such as planning, health and safety, lighting, aesthetics and themes are discussed.

Part III 'Curriculum development' begins with Chapter 8 'Curriculum development in the MSE'. For some children to achieve an appropriate education the regular curriculum may need to be augmented or even replaced. Curriculum options include, from social justice, the compensatory, opposi-tional and counter-hegemonic curricula, and from special education, the sup-ported, modified and alternative curricula. Particular emphasis is placed on the open minded MSE curriculum being outcome-based, individualised and informed by ongoing, meticulous assessment. Chapter 9 'Children with a learning difficulty' provides an account of the ways the MSE might be used to teach a child with a severe learning difficulty to maximise effective use of available vision and hearing. In this chapter MSE curriculum development options for six learning difficulties (visual impairment, hearing impairment, physical disability, intellectual disability, communication disorder, behavioural–emotional disorder) are suggested. In Chapter 10 'Children with severe/profound multiple learning difficulties', MSE curriculum development options are described for such children. Due to the extreme challenge of providing a successful curriculum for children with severe/profound multiple learning difficulties, the MSE curriculum may need to be more targeted, flexible and eclectic than those used in the past. Such a curriculum may need to embrace elements, as and when required, from the developmental, adaptive behaviour and environmental/ecological approaches. Furthermore, a wide range of pedagogical approaches may need to be used (passive, active, child- led and teacher-led).

The final section, Part IV 'Future developments', consists of two chapters. The goal of Chapter 11 'Conducting research in the MSE' is to demystify research and thereby encourage all members of the transdisciplinary team to become actively involved in MSE related research. The aim of this chapter is to provide clear guidelines regarding how to get started and what approaches might be suitable when conducting research. One particular approach, action research, seeks to improve the way the MSE is being used, through collaborative critical self-reflection, monitoring and revision. In Chapter 12 'Where are we going?', the MSE is re-examined to identify possible ways this development could contribute to the increased pluralities that will constitute education in the twenty-first century.

Paul Pagliano
Townsville
August 1998

PART I:
Foundations

Chapter 1

What is a multisensory environment?

Introduction

I asked a teacher who has worked extensively in a multisensory environment (MSE) to describe the MSE in her own words.

'I tend to freak out when people ask me that', she said, 'because I find it really difficult to know how to start to answer. There are so many things I want to say about it – all at once.'

'You mean it's different things to different people?' I enquired.

'That's true, I suppose – but it's more complicated than that. It's almost like there are two different multisensory environments. There's the actual space – the physical environment – and then there's the impact on the students – with this impact being different for each student. If I describe the physical environment it gives a false impression because the physical environment is just a small part. It's somehow too concrete and something qualitative is lost in the process. Then again if I describe the metaphysical there's the opposite problem. The description is too abstract, too abstruse.'

'Well then, could you describe the MSE in two parts beginning with the physical environment?'

The actual space

'Of course you realise that every MSE is different. Our MSE was constructed on a shoestring budget with a lot of goodwill from capable friends who volunteered their time and expertise. We have a principal with good community liaison skills and when a local disco was refurbishing, we were in the right place at the right time. The actual MSE is in an air conditioned converted double classroom. It's pitch black with the lights off and the door closed, although the ceiling, walls and floor have been painted white to provide a neutral three dimensional ground. We could have painted the walls black to create a dark room but we decided to go with the white.

A variety of equipment is on hand to provide visual, auditory, olfactory, tactile and kinesthetic stimulation. These stimuli include a wide range of pleasant aromas, soothing music, vibrating cushions, tactile wall panels, wind chimes, wooden flying birds, beanbags, a water bed, a ball pit, and two giant clear perspex pillars of water with ever-rising air bubbles. A wheel-effect optikinetics projector makes fluid oil patterns that slowly slide across two walls. A touch-responsive plasma light sculpture sits invitingly in one corner and a fibre optic spray cascades light-like water down another. Two spotlights shine on a first clockwise then anticlockwise rotating disco mirror ball while ultraviolet light bounces off neon iridescent flowers, earth globe mobiles, stars and planets, and long hanging coloured tapes. There is a sound system and a television with VCR (video cassette recorder) facilities. When everything is activated it's quite awe-inspiring.'

The impact on the child

'Now can you tell me a story to illustrate the impact your MSE has on one of your students?'

'One girl in my class is called Zoe. She's fifteen. She lives in a small residential setting. They take the best care they can of her but the human resources there are too limited to allow them to give her sustained close individualised attention. Her world is very narrow and she's had a lot of problems. She is extremely tactile defensive. Anything that is put on her tray she will immediately swipe off. She doesn't want anything or anyone to come near her.

Zoe makes a very loud screech like a cockatoo. The screech doesn't change and it's often difficult to identify why she is making a noise. It may be excitement, or pain, or someone or something is too near her, or for no identifiable reason. With pain, if it's really bad she will cry. Most often though the screeching is her letting us know very explicitly that she is not happy with something that is happening.

The interesting point is, she doesn't ever make these noises in the MSE. She seems very happy just being there. I think the MSE has provided her with a sense of security. She has dislocated hips and she's very restricted in her movement. She is often in a lot of pain. She can't be positioned because it would be too painful but she's just capable of moving into a comfortable situation herself. In the ball pit she has no difficulties getting comfortable, and that development, just in itself, is a giant step forward. For the ball pit we plan to gradually take balls out and add different textured objects, to design a more diverse environment just for Zoe. By we I mean the physiotherapist, the occupational therapist, the communication therapist, the teacher's aide and myself. We work together as a team.

We plan to seat her in a beanbag under the fibre optics next to someone she likes. She is starting to like looking at the fibre optics but she doesn't like to touch them. In the beanbag she will be able to observe the other student enjoying touching the fibre optics and we're hoping that in the future she'll more readily allow people and things into her personal space. We'll just have to take it very gradually.

She is very fussy about the types of food and drinks she will accept. She can hold the spoon but needs help to get it into her mouth. If she doesn't like the smell of something she will rub it across her teeth on the spoon and refuse to eat. Recently, however, she has increased her tolerance. What we do is give her something she likes during one session and something she's not so keen on, but is nice, at a second session later during the day. If she refuses that's fine. For a long time before we started going to the MSE there was no progress at all. So now I feel we are making progress, even if it's slow. After she has had lots of positive experiences in the ball pit we'll see how she reacts to a different setting.'

'So in summary you feel Zoe's unique relationship with the MSE provides you with an expanded range of options. You then carefully orchestrate these options to create a learning, therapeutic and recreational environment in which Zoe can interact with the world in new and constructive ways.'

'That's the idea. It's complicated though.'

(Parts of this transcript appeared in Pagliano 1997a).

History

Three separate factors, all of which began development in the 1970s, can be seen as major technological and sociological contributions to the evolution of the MSE. It was the birth of the discotheque with its focus on visual and aural ambience, the popularisation of soft play constructions in early childhood centres and the radical revision of expectations in the provision of services for individuals with disabilities that were pivotal (Hirstwood and Gray 1995).

The discotheque phenomenon is continuing to sweep and re-sweep the western world. The discotheque environment relies on loud rhythmic music and sophisticated, synchronised, sound-activated lighting and special effects to set the scene. All over the world designers have vied with each other to create ever more exciting entertainment spaces. In the process useful lessons have been learnt in applying industrial psychology to MSE design. A further facet of the discotheque phenomenon is the disc jockey, an individual who not only chooses how and when to play the dance music but also skilfully manipulates the extra-aural environment. Through microtechnological developments it has become possible to create interesting portable sound and lighting systems comparatively easily and cheaply. The discotheque phenomenon however is not only technological but also sociological with regard to the semiotics of youth culture (Woodill 1994) .

The popularisation of soft play constructions for use in early childhood also began in the 1970s. An increasing demand for institutional childcare resulted in the emergence of a powerful and influential childcare industry. Many early childhood centres wanted all-weather play environments that were safe, stimulating, attractive and easy to keep clean and maintain. New synthetic materials appeared on the market which could be used to cover foam rubber to make lightweight, waterproof, sturdy shapes. These shapes could be used for manipulation, relaxation and exercise including climbing, jumping, rolling and sliding, and could be made in a wide range of attractive colours. The addition of Velcro meant these large solid shapes could be arranged and rearranged in stable yet innovative ways. Additional developments have included other plastic environmental toys such as building blocks, ladders, tubes, chutes and ball pits. This revolution has been so pervasive that even shopping centres nowadays frequently have a soft toy play centre to entertain the children while the parents are busy shopping.

Services for individuals with disabilities have undergone considerable change since the 1970s. Three early developments were normalisation, the goal of making the life of the individual with a disability as normal as possible (Bank-Mikkelson 1969), de-institutionalisation, the process of moving individuals with disabilities out of institutions into the community (Wolfensberger 1972) and mainstreaming, the process of moving children with disabilities out of segregated special schools into regular education. Kirk and Gallagher (1989) claimed that during this period the field of special education changed perspective moving 'from a **medical model**, which implies a physical condition or disease within a patient, to an **ecological model**, in which we see the exceptional child in complex interaction with environmental forces' (p. 6).

Fulcher (1989) argued this change in perspective is discourse related. 'Discourses articulate the world in certain ways: they "identify" "problems", perspectives on those problems and thus "solutions"' (p. 8). She suggested that two opposing sets of discourses were at play, namely 'divisive' and 'inclusive', 'professionalism' and 'democratism' (p. 9).

> . . . crudely put, the divisive discourse theorizes problems as belonging to the child and as therefore 'needing' extra resources, whereas the inclusive discourse suggests the school has a responsibility to treat all children firstly as pupils, and therefore to concentrate on pedagogical solutions to do with curriculum which all teachers might use (p. 9) . . . . Democratism is the view that those affected by decisions should take a genuine part in debating the issues and in making these decisions. Democratization is the historical struggle in which democratism has been the key strategy. Professionalism, the view that experts know best, has been the major tactic in professionalization, the historical struggle to gain control of an area of occupational life. (p. 15)

A range of discourses are now acknowledged as being influential in disability services. Fulcher's (1989) 'rights discourse' with its themes of 'self-reliance, independence, consumer wants (rather than needs)' (p. 30) has played an important role in the development of the MSE. However, the medical model and discourse have not been entirely discarded. This point will be further developed in Chapters 2 and 5.

Early MSEs combined a visual and aural ambience with soft play constructions to create an environment where the wishes of the individual with a disability determined the activity. Consequently more subtle forms of communication based on the individual's attention, interest and expressions of pleasure or displeasure began to emerge as the basis for participation in the MSE. These early MSEs were called 'snoezelens'.

From snoezelen to multisensory environment

Following on from these three developments, and against a background of increasingly prevalent education research *per se*, environmental factors influencing students with disabilities started to be investigated. Cleland and Clark (1966) described a 'sensory cafeteria' (p. 213) in which a variety of sensory stimulations elicited a variety of responses. This can be regarded as the progenitor of the MSE. Hulsegge and Verheul extended the 'sensory cafeteria' idea in *Snoezelen: Another World* (1986 Dutch, 1987 English) to establish an early MSE.

The word 'snoezelen' was a contraction of two Dutch words meaning to smell and to doze. Over a period of more than seven years Hulsegge and Verheul had created a series of sensory rooms (tactile, aural, visual, ball bath, water, smell and taste) at the De Hartenberg Centre in The Netherlands. These rooms provided relaxation and stimulation for individuals of all ages (particularly adults with intellectual disability). Hulsegge and Verheul also reported on similar rooms, built throughout The Netherlands and Belgium, that were successfully being used with individuals with dementia, mental health problems and a wide range of disabilities.

> Snoezelen has given us the means to provide a wide range of sensory experiences that increase the quality of life of the individual. It also allows us to provide meaningful activity without the need for intellectual or developmental pursuits. (Kewin 1994a, p. 8)

By the late 1980s MSEs appeared in a number of countries throughout Europe. They were built in the UK in a wide range of settings from homes, to schools through to large residential institutions. Their main uses continued to be recreational and therapeutic but some educational uses were appearing in the literature. One particular well documented MSE, described as a suite of rooms for adult users, was located at Whittington Hall Hospital in Chesterfield, Derbyshire (Hutchinson 1991). By the early 1990s MSEs for use in education had appeared in countries around the world including those in Australasia, Africa and the Middle East. By the mid to late 1990s MSEs had been established throughout Canada and the USA (Quon 1998).

'Snoezelen' became the registered trade mark for a UK company ROMPA marketing MSE equipment. This company dominated MSE development for several years, although now a variety of other companies also manufacture and market MSE equipment. In order to avoid association with any commercial interests, the term 'snoezelen' was discarded in the literature and the term 'multisensory environment' was adopted instead. Unshackling the MSE from the narrow definition imposed by commercial interests resulted in a freeing up of the use of the MSE, especially in the education of children with disabilities.

Mount and Cavet (1995) called for increased critical evaluation of the MSE in the field of special education: 'The expansion and popularity . . . has led us to ask, what are multi-sensory environments and how can their usefulness be evaluated?' (p. 52). The popularity of MSEs is continuing to grow and it is of concern that comparatively little specific research to directly inform and guide MSE use has appeared in the professional literature.

Running in tandem with MSE developments, however, is a rich vein of educational research that relates to sensory development (Barraga 1964; Ayres 1979; Nielsen 1979, 1991, 1992a,b; Longhorn 1988) and the education of children with severe/profound multiple disabilities. (The contributions made by a number of researchers will be examined in Chapter 3.) Linking this voluminous indirect research to the direct MSE research (see Chapter 2) has helped to develop a theoretical base to predicate MSE use.

Philosophy of the 'snoezelen'

Hulsegge and Verheul (1986/7) made important early attempts to formulate a system of values to underpin use of the MSE. Their 'snoezelen' philosophy was developed from working in a residential institution with individuals of all ages, but was more related to recreation and leisure for adults than to education for children. Consequently when their philosophy was adopted primarily for use in education, serious criticisms emerged (Mount and Cavet 1995). These criticisms included the lack of research data to inform MSE use, the need to depend on staff intuition to achieve success, the question of compatibility of MSEs with inclusion (Whittaker 1992) and whether artifical MSEs numb 'our capacity to recognise the multisensory nature of all . . . places' (Orr 1993, p. 26).

Hulsegge and Verheul's (1986/7) snoezelen philosophy was founded on the premise that for an individual with severe/profound disability, an appeal to primary sensations was a more immediately powerful means of contact than any initial appeal to intellectual capabilities. Learning was regarded as secondary or incidental. 'Learning is not a must, but they [the individuals with severe/profound disability] should be given the opportunity to gain experience. . . . if he [or she] learns something in the process, that is a bonus' (p. 23). There was stress on the 'beneficial effect on mutual trust' and also the idea that MSEs require 'careful observation [of the person with severe/profound disability] . . . in order to recognize, register and translate signals' (p. 126).

The Hulsegge and Verheul vision was of an environment where the person with a disability was in control, where the professional, parent or carer was there as a facilitator – someone to watch closely and to act responsively in order to ensure that the environment matched the mood of the individual user. They stressed the need for facilitators to be discriminating, to adopt a 'critical attitude' (p. 10) and to make decisions for themselves. In practice though facilitations tended to be narrow because there was no exploration beyond the bounds of the philosophy. The facilitator was given formal 'training' and rules of what was and what was not permissable in a MSE. The ecological approach was partly embraced but the medical model traditions were deeply ingrained.

Hulsegge and Verheul criticised their own work stating that it lacked 'a solid theoretical basis' to guide and inform MSE use. Furthermore, they stated that their philosophy lacked 'uniformity' (p. 127). Despite these shortfalls the work of Hulsegge and Verheul captured the imagination of many professionals who took up the challenge and established their own MSEs in a wide range of therapeutic, recreational and educational settings.

The combined approach

Educational use of the MSE in the UK resulted in the regular appearance of two diametrically opposed approaches in the MSE literature. Hirstwood and Smith (1996) explain how the two approaches developed:

> There has been to date a philosophical rivalry within multi-sensory approaches that has polarized much of the work. The multi-sensory movement regularly cites the Hartenburg Institute as its birth place. The concept of Snoezelen ... was developed and refined there, and underlies much of what could be termed the passive approach. However, during the same period, the growth of microtechnology was prompting an increase in switching as a discrete skill. From a variety of sources switches that could control mains-operated devices such as lights and tape recorders were developed. This route has been refined and developed into what is often termed the interactive approach. (p. 84)

Bozic (1997a) isolated these two distinct interpretative repertoires or approaches using discourse analysis on interview transcripts of staff from four special schools. The 'child-led repertoire' or passive approach described a room that was comfortable, gentle, quiet and warm where emphasis was placed on positive, emotional reactions. Decisions were made by the child who relaxed while the adult remained physically close by. The 'developmental repertoire' or interactive approach described a room that was stimulating, where the child developed through levels, with the teacher supplying the direction, where the child was active and emphasis was placed on individually tailored experiences.

Hirstwood and Smith (1996) argued that these two approaches could be used together to provide a richer more flexible educational environment:

> In our experience these approaches are compatible, and children will not only benefit from aspects of each, but should be given the opportunity to

work in both modes if they are to gain fully from the advantages of multi-sensory technology. Multi-sensory rooms are places where teachers can control the child's environment closely; places where they can create the specific setting that they want for each individual. (p. 84)

The combined approach method considerably widens the repertoire of ways in which the MSE can be used. Such a marriage of philosophies helps to address criticisms that were lodged at the original passive approach (lack of research data to inform MSE use, need to depend on staff intuition to achieve success, compatibility of MSEs with inclusion and whether artificial MSEs numb capacity to recognise the multisensory nature of all places).

The flexibility of the combined approach makes it easier to conduct research in the MSE. 'Research does not inevitably constrain or distort the evaluation of naturalistic or self-directed and spontaneous activity and should in fact contribute to the refinement and development of provision' (Glen *et al.* 1996, p. 72). Research-derived knowledge (see Chapter 11), transdisciplinary collaboration (see Chapter 5) and interpersonal problem-solving (see Chapter 7) all lessen the need for reliance on staff intuition.

The combined approach provides a rationale for MSEs being compatible with inclusion. The MSE can become a place for the congregation of children with disabilities or a place where non-disabled children visit with children with disabilities. Pagliano (1997a, p. 79) reported on a physiotherapist who argued that in the MSE the children with disabilities are 'at their best'. Consequently the MSE is an excellent place for children with disabilities to meet with non-disabled children.

We have a very unusual population of children. We would like other people to see our children at their best – especially because the children are difficult to communicate with. If parents and non-disabled brothers and sisters [and friends] see the children happy, laughing and relaxed, as they so often are in the . . . [MSE], they're going to relate to them more than if they see them cranky, throwing their arms and legs around, dribbling and angry. Unfortunately that's the way they usually are when they see them in the outside world. (Therapist)

Far from numbing capacity to recognise the multisensory nature of all places the combined MSE approach actually serves to accentuate multisensory experience in the real world by providing renewed opportunities for generalisation from the constructed to the natural environment (see Chapter 3).

A definition of the MSE

The MSE is virtually impossible to define precisely. Any environment is multisensory to a greater or lesser degree. The MSE is conventionally defined in terms of a specific type of physical environment but this ignores other even more important though nebulous aspects. Functional definitions relating to leisure, skill development and learning are similarly incomplete.

A constellation of MSE apparatus and resources can be described (see Chapter 4) but the concrete nature of the MSE is only a part of its definition. Rather it is the type, level and combination of sensations that are sufficient to rouse an individual's interest that is relevant. Such an individual's response is tempered by intrinsic and extrinsic factors and can vary from day to day. Hence the same physical environment has multiple realities for a variety of users and for each of its users.

The MSE is not fixed, but is in dynamic equilibrium with its user. The fullest definition of the MSE can only be determined by that user at that time. The expanded remit of the combined approach gives an indication of how broad this wide interpretation of the MSE can be. In essence

> the new MSE is a dedicated space or room for relaxation and/or work, where stimulation can be controlled, manipulated, intensified, reduced, presented in isolation or combination, packaged for active or passive interaction, and temporally matched to fit the perceived motivation, interests, leisure, relaxation, therapeutic and/or educational needs of the user. It can take a variety of physical, psychological and sociological forms. (Pagliano 1998a)

An educational definition of the MSE must begin with the individual child. The MSE only has value as an educational tool if it is meaningful to the child in positive ways. Without this the room itself is of little value.

Figure 1.1   Drawing of a MSE by a five-year-old child

Chapter 2

Survey of the MSE literature

Introduction

The first substantial use of the multisensory environment (MSE), as a recreational and, to a much lesser extent, therapeutic and educational tool, was in The Netherlands. Hulsegge and Verheul's (1986/7) 'snoezelen' philosophy developed from their work in residential institutions with adults and children with profound intellectual and multiple disabilities. Their goal was to create a user-controlled, safe, appropriate leisure environment for relaxation and/or stimulation by appealing to primary sensations. Learning and therapy were regarded as incidental. When asked the question 'Is 'snoezelen' aimed at relaxation or is it therapy?' Hulsegge and Verheul replied 'We wish to regard 'snoezelen' primarily as a form of relaxation' (p. 121).

The ensuing wide acceptance of the beneficial nature of the MSE, by leisure, therapy and education practitioners, is largely predicated on faith and optimism (Slane 1993; Mount and Cavet 1995). Until recently there has been little formal evaluation of the MSE in the research literature nor informed debate of its strengths and limitations. Most research has been subjective and descriptive. There are several reasons for practitioners' relative lack of research endeavour. They include lack of perception that research is indeed necessary, lack of agreement regarding what should be researched, lack of experience using appropriate methodologies and lack of resources especially time and money.

Checking assumptions

MSEs 'were originally developed within a philosophical framework which emphasized that it was acceptable to develop an environment which promoted service users' pleasure for its own sake', therefore research was thought to be an imposition (Cavet and Mount 1995, p. 82). Hutchinson and Haggar (1991) in particular argued against conducting outcome orientated research stating 'It is hoped that future workers in the field will not feel obliged to justify the existence of Snoezelen purely in terms of therapeutic outcome . . . "Do we justify our own leisure pursuits in terms of their therapeutic value?"' If the

MSE's principal function is as a place for leisure and recreation for people with disabilities, to research the therapeutic value of the MSE would alter the emphasis and the approach.

The anti-research argument has strongly influenced the way MSEs have been used in both education and the therapies. Glen *et al.* (1996) explain

> There is some resistance to research and formal evaluations of these environments on the grounds that this would force the clients into more structured, outcome-oriented work. In other words, the emphasis would be on work (by definition set from outside the individual), in contrast to play and freely chosen leisure . . . Furthermore, whilst no one disputes the importance of play and self-selected activities for young, normally developing children, all too often activities for those with disabilities have to be justified on therapeutic or educational grounds. The emphasis is frequently on teacher-selected, goal oriented activities which are often then teacher-led, and this in turn is likely to reduce child control and spontaneity. (p. 72)

Lack of agreement regarding what should be researched results from a range of opinion on how the MSE should be used. Some therapists consider that the MSEs should be used as 'safe havens' where emphasis is on free choice and leisure. Other therapists consider that the MSEs should be used as environments for learning skills (Thompson and Martin 1994). A parallel issue has emerged in special education literature in terms of the desirability of 'passive' versus 'interactive' approaches (National Council for Educational Technology 1993; Hirstwood and Smith 1996; Bozic 1997a).

Evidently there are differing assumptions being made regarding what constitutes a MSE. One assumption comes from the 'snoezelen' philosophy approach. Here the assumption is that the MSE is for leisure and relaxation for individuals with disabilities. Another assumption relates to the use of therapy, namely that the environment be used for therapy to develop skills. Another assumption is that the environment be used to promote learning. Finally, there is a fourth group who assume that the MSE can be multifunctional, that there is no need for any of the above interpretations, because the use is determined by the user.

Unfortunately research to inform these assumptions has not been regarded as a high priority. Instead often anecdotal experience couched in the ideology of the speaker has been given credence and allowed to fill the vacuum:

> it is surprising that such facilities [MSEs] are widely used, often without either a consistent approach among staff or any prior scientific evaluation. This is especially surprising in light of the scientific rigour imposed on most other areas of client related work. (Thompson and Martin 1994, pp. 341–2)

The importance of using appropriate methodologies to investigate the MSE is paramount. In order for this to happen each researcher must check what assumptions are being made when defining the purpose of the MSE being investigated and then develop a research paradigm to suit the assumption.

Four themes

The MSE literature can be divided into four themes, where each theme describes a particular type of MSE. The MSE in the first theme closely follows the original 'Snoezelen philosophy'. This MSE is created principally for the leisure and recreation of individuals with disabilities. The MSE in the second theme has been developed principally for therapy, specifically designed for the treatment of some disorder or condition. The MSE in the third theme has been principally created for education, to promote learning and development. The MSE in the fourth theme is multifunctional. This space can be used for leisure and recreation, for therapy, for education, or for any permutation and combination of the three. It is a 'living environment' where there is a tenuous relationship between constancy and change, where the environment is determined by the needs of the user and shaped by the intelligence and sensitivity of the transdisciplinary team that manage it.

The classification of the MSE as a particular type of space that is determined by its function and design is based on ideas expressed in political theory and architecture. Rogers (1997) explains in relation to urban space

> The political theorist Michael Walzer classified urban space into two distinct groups: 'single-minded' and 'open-minded' spaces. 'Single-minded' describes a concept of urban space that fulfils a single function and is generally the consequence of decisions by old-guard planners or developers. 'Open-minded' is conceived as multi-functional and has evolved or been designed for a variety of uses in which everyone can participate. (p. 13)

MSEs that have been developed for a single function or purpose, namely those in the first three themes, are analogous to Walzer's 'single-minded' space classification. MSEs that have been developed for many different functions, namely those in the fourth theme, are analogous to Walzer's 'open-minded' space classification. Rogers argues that while 'single-minded' spaces 'cater to our modern craving for private consumption and autonomy' they are counter to the concept of inclusion. Alternatively 'open-minded' spaces promote inclusion because they 'bring diverse sections of society together and breed a sense of tolerance, awareness, identity and mutual respect' (p. 13).

The MSE concept began as a 'single-minded' space because it was specifically designed to cater for the enjoyment of individuals with disabilities. Through a process of morphogenesis the original concept spawned new 'single-minded' space interpretations where the goal was either that of therapy or education. Inevitably where the MSE took on the role of a place for leisure, therapy or education, there were arguments regarding the primary purpose of the MSE (Thompson and Martin 1994; Hirstwood and Smith 1996; Bozic 1997a). With the advent of the transdisciplinary team, especially in the field of inclusive education for children with disabilities, professionals began to collaborate. In the process, the 'single-minded' MSE space of the past was transformed into an 'open-minded' space and arguments regarding the single purpose of the MSE became redundant.

Theme one: the MSE based on the 'Snoezelen philosophy'

As discussed previously there has been a tendency for MSEs based on the 'snoezelen' philosophy not to be formally researched. Literature written about this type of MSE is largely descriptive with the focus on design, what equipment to include and how to train staff to use the facility. The principal focus has been leisure and recreation for individuals with disabilities – although in some cases there is some secondary movement towards the use of the MSE for therapy.

Hutchinson (1991) edited a collection of papers describing the 'Whittington Hall Snoezelen Project', a leisure and recreation facility established in 1990, for people with 'severe learning difficulties' (Kewin 1991a,b,c; Cunningham *et al.* 1991; Hutchinson and Haggar 1991). A change was made at the hospital from the traditional 'activity base' to 'sensory experience' (Kewin 1991a). Observations were made of 14 clients using 'six specially adapted areas' (1) adventure room (2) jacuzzi (3) sitting room (4) sound and light room (5) touch corridor, and (6) white room. Clients found the environment relaxing, stimulating and enjoyable. Professionals recorded reductions in maladaptive behaviour (Cunningham *et al* 1991). Hutchinson and Haggar (1991; 1994) concluded that 'it appears to be working for them' (Haggar and Hutchinson 1991).

Kewin (1991b) identified an important additional benefit as the carer/participant relationship itself:

> As relationships between users and helpers develop within Snoezelen and we focus more on sensory experience and communication, there can be a freeing up of carer/participant relationships. People are more readily accepted as interesting individuals in their own right as we learn much more about their likes and dislikes.

Rather than the passive positioning of the participant prevalent in the medical model, here the participant is more actively involved. The snoezelen philosophy therefore encourages the recognition of the potentiality of the individual.

The MSE at Botleys Park was described by Long and Haig (1992) as a 'cocoon-like atmosphere' for individuals who 'normally find conventional therapeutic and leisure activities difficult to access intellectually' (p. 103). Their guiding objective was to provide a stimulating, secure atmosphere, to heighten awareness, promote exploration, relaxation, freedom and social inter- action. Research was conducted to see if MSE activities for four clients would result in observable changes in behaviour. Results after six months were encouraging with the objectives reported as 'apparently' being met (p. 106).

Research in Southampton by psychologists Thompson and Martin (1994) involved six clients (three male, three female) with moderate learning disabil- ities (age range 26–32 years). Each keyworker was given a preference assessment form to identify possible reinforcers for each client. Results consisted of a unique individual hierarchy of preferred responses for each client. This preference profile was then available to inform individualised MSE use. Outcomes were not recorded. Such an individualised approach however has great value as a basis for curriculum development for children with learning difficulties (see Part III).

Henning (1994) investigated the use of 'Snoezelen techniques and philoso- phies' with individuals 'with profound intellectual disabilities who display self-injurious behaviour' (p. 109). She argued that while MSE use is not a 'panacea' it does offer some individuals a 'mini vacation' from their cycle of self-injury, even if the effects of the MSE cannot be shown to generalise to other environments. Henning listed eight suggestions for use in the MSE with children with profound intellectual disability who display self-injurious behaviour. They are:

1. Be aware that individuals who self-injure may experience difficulty adapting to new people as well as to new situations.
2. Gently introduce the MSE with the client as the only participant.
3. Respect the client's personal space, introduce touch gradually and only with the client's approval.
4. Be aware restraints may or may not provide a sense of security, lotions may have negative or positive associations.
5. Allow the client to lead, set the pace, share (respect the client's privacy at all times).
6. Match goals to needs, keep precise measurements, if formally recorded these can be part of an individualised education plan (IEP).
7. Identify reasons for self-injury by conducting a functional analysis (could include stress, depression, too much or too little stimulation, difficulty with personal relationships, frustration with communication).
8. If self-injury is directly related to seizure, use MSE in close consultation with medical practitioner.

Ashby *et al.* (1995) reported on a study at Strathmartine Hospital involving six females and two males (aged 23 to 62 years) with profound and multiple disabilities. All individuals were residents of the same hospital ward. The researchers investigated the effects on concentration and responsiveness of

these individuals after 20 MSE sessions each of 20 minutes duration
conducted over a three-week period. Assessment of concentration consisted
of each individual being asked to complete a simple shape board puzzle. All
meaningful movements towards engaging in the task were scored.

Assessment of responsiveness consisted of video taping of the 1st, 5th,
10th, 15th and 20th session and points were scored for the individual's
enjoyment, relaxation and comfort. Results were reported as individual case
studies. They indicated that seven of the eight individuals responded in some
positive way. Improvements in concentration were substantial for two,
moderate for four and minimal for one. While changes in concentation were
not always related to MSE responsiveness/enjoyment the two individuals who
showed the greatest gains in concentration were also rated as being the most
responsive in the MSE.

Theme two: the MSE designed for therapy

Research has been conducted by therapists in the MSE investigating its use
with a wide variety of clients including those who have problems that are not
traditionally included under the disability banner.

Moffat et al. (1993) traced the use of sensory stimulation with adults with
dementia back to the late 1950s. Liederman et al. (1958) argued that some
patients' problems may be caused by the sensorily deprived settings in which
they lived. This idea was supported by Solomon et al. (1961) who demonstrated that individuals suffered adverse effects when placed in sensorily-
deprived environments. Six years later, Bower (1967) investigated in a
controlled trial two groups of 25 individuals with dementia. One group
received stimulation for four and a half hours, five days a week, and a control
group received no stimulation. After six months two thirds of individuals in
the control group had deteriorated whereas individuals in the stimulation
group either remained unchanged or showed improvement.

MSE use with patients with dementia began in The Netherlands, possibly
because nursing homes employed activity coordinators whose job description
included finding ways to occupy patients' time. Little research literature is
available on Dutch developments. Bloemhard (1992) suggested MSE use
helped reduce staff burn-out because it provided a pleasant way to get to
know patients particularly those with severe communication disorders.

Moffat et al. (1993) pioneered MSE dementia research in the UK with six
long-stay and six day patients at King's Park Community Hospital,
Bournemouth. Patients attended MSE sessions of 30 minutes, three times a
week for four weeks. Comparison of before- and after-session ratings of
happiness and interest showed an increase. During the four-week period the
number of patients who remained calm and showed interest throughout a
session also increased. However, no evidence of any generalisation of the

benefits to other aspects of mood and behaviour were observed. Researchers concluded that the 'experience of carrying out . . . [MSE] sessions with patients with dementia has been generally positive' (p. 30).

Further work at the same hospital was reported by Pinkney and Barker (1994). Particular adaptations to suit this population were described, including ideas for room design and equipment based on principles of safety, comfort and familiarity, ideas with regard to attention to timing and content, when, how long and how to introduce and conclude the MSE activity. The authors claimed that MSE use for this population was 'developing its own approach, style and therapeutic outcome' (p. 181).

Pinkney (1997) also reported on a study where a comparison was made between the MSE and a music relaxation group on the mood and behaviour of three patients with senile dementia at King's Park Community Hospital. Results indicated that both approaches were 'equally effective at manipulating mood and affect in a positive way. However, each . . . possesses powerful stimuli that may be used to select certain responses' (p. 212). The music group was useful in stimulating musical memory whereas the MSE offered a more global stimulation which could be adapted to match particular needs and situations. Pinkney concluded that 'Nothing therapeutic may be gained by indiscriminately placing individuals in a room waiting for something to happen. The most successful experience may be gained by selecting the appropriate combination of stimulation for each individual' (p. 212).

A more recent King's Park study was reported by Baker et al. (1997). They investigated the long- and short-term effects on older people with dementia using a randomised controlled trial involving 31 (16 male, 15 female) patients. The effects of eight standardised MSE sessions were compared with a 'credible control condition of eight standardised activity sessions' (p. 214). Care was taken to ensure that MSE and activity sessions were very similar. These included the equivalent number and length of sessions, staff–patient contact time, assessments, level of skill and preparation including emphasis placed on both approaches being framed as positive activities.

In contrast to Moffat et al. (1993), Baker et al. (1997) found evidence of generalisation of benefits to other aspects and behaviour. Socially-disturbed behaviour improved significantly in the home setting over the trial. This result led the authors to suggest that 'Perhaps regular exposure to the unique Snoezelen environment has a normalising effect on patients' (p. 217). In line with findings reported by Bower (1967) deviant behaviour at the day hospital remained the same, whereas for the control group it deteriorated significantly. This result led the authors to suggest that 'Perhaps the Snoezelen environment is more effective in preventing an increase in deviant behaviour within the general deteriorating pattern of dementia' (p. 217).

Four patients in this study disliked the room so much their sessions were not continued. The authors reported that one patient found the room claustrophobic and became quite anxious on entry, and the remaining three patients expressed a distinct dislike for the room. However, two of these participants were viewed by staff to be generally intolerant of most interventions or interactions beyond their daily routine during that period of time. (p. 217)

This prompted the authors to state 'It certainly appears that the Snoezelen environment, at least in its white room form, is not for everyone' (p. 217).

Smith and McAllister (1994) reported on white room MSE use as an alternative to traditional methods of relaxation for adults with depressive and anxiety-related mental health difficulties at the Psychiatric Day Unit, Chesterfield Royal Hospital. MSE benefits identified were:

1. alleviation of anxiety about joining group relaxation;
2. helping individuals with acute mental health problems feel safe;
3. suiting deaf individuals;
4. concentrating on the immediate present; and
5. pressure and intensity in learning techniques were reduced.

Relaxation seemed to be achieved because the pressure to concentrate and participate was removed, individuals were free to choose activities in a 'time out' environment where the gentle stimulation offered distraction from stressful situations. MSE activities helped caseworkers establish rapport with clients and in some situations helped with counselling. The MSE was identified as an important treatment choice for individuals facing a crisis situation.

Another study conducted by Scholfield (1994) investigated the use of the MSE with individuals with chronic pain. Often individuals with chronic pain find that the pain and its repercussions tower over all other aspects of daily life. Depression is common. The MSE in its various forms, through stimulation and relaxation, can provide an opportunity for improved carer relationships, the successful integration of many pain management approaches including assessment (psychological and physical), diagnostic procedures, physical, occupational, massage, family therapy, psychological treatment, nerve block/trigger injections, acupuncture, relaxation 'training' and education.

Theme three: the MSE designed for education

When MSEs first appeared in The Netherlands they served an important new function in the care of children with severe multiple disabilities. Hulsegge and Verheul (1986/7) explain

Many parents of ... children [with severe disabilities] ... thought: 'My child is incapable of anything!' This feeling of impotence was amplified by the fact that eight years ago parents did not have a say in the care of their child. . . . 'Snoezelen' is an activity where 'expertise' is not absolutely necessary, it is an emotional affair not requiring years of training. (p. 116)

This interpretation provided commercial companies with an attractive marketing strategy. The strategy that expertise was not essential meant that the MSE could be aimed directly at the lay public, especially parents who wanted to care for their child at home, instead of placing their child in an institution and leaving everything to the 'experts' as had previously been the expectation.

Further interest was generated by the argument that the child be in control. At this time concern was being voiced in the literature that the use of direct instruction approaches in the education of children with severe learning difficulties encouraged a dependency relationship where the teacher owned the learning – not the child (Mithaug *et al.* 1988; Mithaug 1991). The trouble with special education, it was argued, is that the child is given too much help and not provided with sufficient opportunities to learn independently. (The issue of self-determination is further developed in Chapters 6 and 10.)

'Snoezelen' is in itself a passive occupation in the sense that no direct exertion is required. . . . Our contribution to it should at first be minimal. We leave the [child] . . . room to decide where he [or she] wishes to sit or lie down. *He* [or she] decides when we go to another place or room . . . whether we can sit down next to him. In a way we depend on *his* [or her] *experience*. (Hulsegge and Verheul 1986/7, p. 117)

This meant that the 'snoezelen' *laissez-faire* philosophy could be viewed as a legitimate educational approach, a sense of self and choice being vital precursors to learning.

The acceptance of the MSE in the UK was supported by the publication of a sensory curriculum by Longhorn (1988). She argued that children with severe and profound multiple disabilities may be unable to learn from general teaching methods because the children were insufficiently aware of the world around them. The non-disabled child develops sense ability spontaneously but children with severe sensory disability may need to have their senses 'awakened' through increased sensory stimulation. Longhorn recommended that teachers carefully assess available space to create environments that 'enable the Sensory Curriculum to be taught effectively' (p. 20).

Despite wide use of MSEs in special schools in the UK in the late 1980s and early 1990s there was little accompanying research. This prompted Mount and Cavet (1995) to write:

There is a danger . . . that in the absence of rigorous research the value of multi-sensory environments will be over-estimated and, in the present situation, may be regarded as active treatment centres when, in fact, they are being used for containment, or as dumping ground where people with learning difficulties are placed and ignored. At best a multi-sensory room can increase the alternatives available to people with profound and multiple learning difficulties and may be motivational for staff. At worst it may divert the attention of staff from recognising the potential for stimulation in everyday environments, and can provide an unstimulating and incomprehensible setting for people with learning difficulties. (p. 54)

Literature has tended to be descriptive or discursive with little direct observational data.

A publication by the National Council for Educational Technology (1993) argued that there were two interpretations for MSEs for children; to foster relaxation and exploration with emphasis 'on developing a person's feeling of autonomy and control' and as a 'tool for perceptual education with clear objectives and outcomes' (p. 2). Switches were thought to provide the child with opportunities for access and control, to in turn promote understanding of 'cause and effect' and to provide opportunities for ongoing monitoring of the child's development. Specific MSE uses identified were to promote:

1. sense development
2. hand–eye coordination
3. appreciation of cause and effect
4. communication development
5. user control
6. relaxation
7. passive stimulation (access to feelings)
8. tools for higher-order learning.

The use of a dedicated space was recommended as was the need for school staff to work out a philosophy that 'best matches . . . aims' with the 'needs of . . . students' (p. 3).

In Hewitt's (1993) study, staff at seven Birmingham schools completed questionnaires on their MSEs. Results showed that a number of different names other than MSE were being used, including 'light room', 'sensory room' and 'interactive learning environment', as well as the commercial names (SNOEZELEN®, White Tower). MSEs at the schools were being used by teachers, physiotherapists, occupational therapists, speech therapists, visiting teachers, students/volunteers and parents. MSE use included sensory work, massage, aromatherapy, drama, movement, relaxation; most staff had received 'training' in these areas. Staff also indicated that they kept records and linked MSE work with the curriculum.

Lister (1993) investigated the use of dark multi-sensory environments (DMSEs) at eight special schools in a local education authority. The DMSE is a development of the original MSE with an overweening emphasis on visual stimulation (see Chapter 6). Ten 19 question surveys were completed (one school had three DMSEs) and revealed the following:

- DMSEs were located in either a classroom, office or walk in cupboard.
- They were used with children with profound multiple learning difficulties, hearing impairments, visual impairments and physical impairments and use ranged from single class to whole school involvement.
- Specific objectives were devised on an individual basis although some group, staff and school guidelines were developed.
- The three schools that had an ultraviolet (UV) light facility described the facility as worthwhile and each school had formed a policy for its usage (see Chapter 7).

An account of setting up and developing a MSE at Limington House School, Hampshire, UK – a special school for children with severe to profound multiple learning difficulties – is provided by Gallagher and Balsom (1994) and de Bunsen (1994). De Bunsen examined the effect of the MSE on six children with 'extreme challenging behaviour' (p. 139). Observations and records were kept over a six-week period (two weeks not using MSE, two weeks using MSE, two weeks not using MSE). The researcher concluded that 'Though I had hoped for a more conclusive and clearly defined result the staff and I feel there are sufficient favourable indications to warrant further investigation' (p. 144). Melberg and Jansson (1994) also described the evolution and use of a MSE with children at a school in Sweden and with no specific data claimed that the children were benefiting. Hirstwood and Gray's (1995) MSE book provides a comprehensive practical guide to the use of multi-sensory rooms for children with disabilities, details what can be included and where this material may be obtained.

Glen et al. (1996) investigated claims that individuals with profound and multiple learning difficulty (PMLD) 'enjoyed the [MSE] ... and returned readily, exercised choice, became more relaxed and showed a reduction in stereotypic behaviour' (p. 72). Their research involved three girls and two boys with PMLD aged between four and 14 years, in the two to nine months developmental range. Children and parents (when possible; some sessions were missed because of illness) spent one hour a week for eight weeks in the MSE. Children spent ten minutes on each of four activities, five minutes with the parent and five minutes alone. Observers recorded child behaviours each fifteen seconds and compared results. After eight weeks both the observers and parents commented on their experiences.

Findings included:

- All involved certainly appeared to enjoy their time in the MSE.
- All the children showed clear preferences for specific activities.
- No one activity was preferred by all children, highlighting the children's individuality and reinforcing the notion that they actively selected their preferences.

- The most disabled children were the most dependent on effecting change in their environment by social means, illustrated by their attempts to re-establish social contact in the alone condition.
- Mothers' comments indicate that many formed new conceptions about their child – often seeing new abilities. (p. 81)

Hirstwood and Smith (1996) described MSEs as 'places where teachers can control the child's environment closely; places where they can create the specific setting that they want for each individual' (p. 84). Reed and Addis (1996) expanded this concept by identifying ways, such as through the use of switches, where a learning environment can be created which enables children to 'explore the notion of control' (p. 92).

Bozic (1997a) used discourse analysis on interview transcripts of staff from four special schoools to identify two distinct approaches that were being used with the MSE in education: a 'child-led repertoire' and a 'developmental repertoire' (p. 57).

The child-led repertoire shares many characteristics with the initial adult-oriented use of multi-sensory rooms ... presented as a comfortable, relaxing place in which children are able to make their own decisions about the activities they become involved in. . . . The developmental repertoire . . . focused on a developmental view of the child progressing through stages and levels. The teacher was depicted as a guiding influence over this progression ... (p. 57)

Bozic's research neatly illustrates the two positions that have been adopted in education, the child-led discovery learning approach and the teacher-led developmental approach. Single-space mindedness is still the predominant paradigm.

Theme four: the MSE as an 'open-minded' space

Gray (1994) in 'A guide to the rooms' implicitly recognises the limitations of a rigid 'single-minded' space. He wrote

Different rooms provide different functions . . .

- White rooms are primarily designed for relaxation and the use of projection. However, they need not be exclusively white, passive or just relaxation orientated environments.
- Dark rooms are primarily designed for visual stimulation and inter-action although again this is not mutually exclusive to this type of room.
- Soft play rooms are designed for boisterous activities such as climbing, bouncing, etc. Again these can be enhanced by using various multi-sensory room equipment components.

- Water rooms, jacuzzi type rooms with multi-sensory equipment are designed for physio/hydrotherapy and relaxation. These are expensive options and not easily justifiable.
- Creative spaces. An empty theatre to be enhanced by imagination or multi-sensory room equipment or both. They promote expression and communication, movement, imaginative creativity. (p. 17)

Bozic and Murdoch (1994) coined the term 'specialized environment' to describe a wide range of environments, including dark rooms (p. 8) and

> 'quiet' rooms and distraction-free areas; little rooms (Nielsen 1988, 1991); multi-sensory rooms; soft play environments; adapted large cupboard boxes and corners of classrooms; massage and amoratherapy (in the sense that they provide olfactory and tactile input, and most specialized environments provide visual and auditory input); resonance boards (Nielsen 1979); circuits (obstacle courses); computers; UV light; soundbeam. (p. 8)

These descriptions open up the MSE to a much wider audience. These environments could be used by practitioners from a range of different disciplines.

A study that clearly moves into Theme Four is that conducted by Pagliano (1997a). His qualitative research at Mundingburra Special School, Townsville, Australia, over a three-year period involved input from an occupational therapist, a physiotherapist and teachers. His research consisted of semi-structured interviews and direct observation of the MSE being used with children with severe multiple disabilities. MSE attributes identified from this research included:

- opportunity for affective/emotional development
- stimulation for all senses
- relaxation
- facilitation of therapy
- enhancement of communication
- minimisation of challenging behaviours
- development of self-determination
- opportunity for social interaction with non-disabled children/families.

However the wealth of information that could be generated from a transdisciplinary approach is yet to be extensively recorded and analysed in a postpositivist paradigm for the literature (see Chapter 11). A multi-faceted dynamic entity needs to be investigated in a way that captures and gives appropriate appraisal to all the facets.

Concerns about the MSE's limitations

Critics of the MSE voiced their concern that an environment specifically designed for the enjoyment and relaxation of individuals with disabilities was segregationalist in nature. Supporters of the MSE counter-argued that the environment's strength lay in the fact that it provided the person with a disability an increased level of self-determination or autonomy.

Moore (1991), an occupational therapist, asked the question 'Whose need is this type of facility actually serving? Is it that of the service users . . . or . . . service providers'. She argued that success might be as much a result of increased social contact as the MSE *per se*. Furthermore

> All of the activities that are offered by a Snoezelen Centre could be found within integrated community facilities. Rather than continuing to provide and develop facilities that ensure that people with learning difficulties remain segregated . . . we should be working with local authorities to provide a 'range of high quality leisure facilities' that are as accessible to people with disabilities as they are to those who are not disabled. (p. 126)

The problem of access to integrated services also troubled Whittaker (1992) who was concerned that the MSE did not appear to prepare the child with disabilities for life in the real world. Orr (1993) agreed, stating 'What is happening is that the behaviour we save for the 'room', is numbing our capacity to recognise the multi-sensory nature of all rooms, all places' (p. 26). Slane (1993) congratulated Orr for 'puncturing of the myth that multi-sensory rooms are automatically good for children. I have my own theory as to why they are spreading so fast. It is because a multi-sensory room is the perfect environment for a stressed teacher' (p. 13).

Hopkins and Willetts (1993) offered further criticism claiming that 'When these places are badly used, the children become passive and confused by competing stimuli, causing them to retreat into a withdrawn state' (p. 26). McLarty (1993) supported the MSE stating that 'the criticism should be of the unimaginative 'professionals' rather than the technology' (p. 11). Gray (1994) agreed, claiming 'we need to focus much more on making sensations meaningful and representative. Rather this than presenting them as "artificial" sensations within a sensory room experience or as a series of sensory assaults during a class session.' (p. 8). For Gray, the biggest problem facing MSEs is the 'lack of transition of skills to other areas' and the second biggest problem is 'people rubbishing a concept that they clearly have not researched in depth or detail' (p. 17).

Research to investigate the strengths and limitations of the MSE is much needed.

Chapter 3

Developing a theoretical perspective of the MSE

... working in a postmodernist age, we should (and largely already do) adjust our actions to meet the specific needs of each individual, recognising the need to be pragmatic and flexible. The therapist needs to be less concerned with a 'distanced and abstract consideration' (Taylor, 1995) and less self-conscious about valuing the subjective. No more is this relevant than in ... learning disability contexts where 'scientific objectivity' and the language of mathematics often finds itself floundering in its attempts to reflect truth or when trying to measure health outcomes. (Webber 1995, p. 440)

Introduction

In Chapter 2 it was indicated that the use of MSEs had gained widespread acceptance in the education of children with learning difficulties, especially profound and multiple learning difficulties, despite there being a small and inconclusive direct research base. All too often MSE use has been based on vague and unsubstantiated claims. A second body of literature is explored in this chapter: non-MSE research information and concepts that could reasonably be used to inform MSE use.

For non-disabled children the world is full of sensory and motor experiences. These experiences trigger spontaneous and innate development of the sensory and motor systems. For many children with disabilities in the sensory or motor areas there is no such guarantee the experiences they receive will promote development. Some children miss out on experiences as a direct consequence of their disability. Others miss out because the available experiences do not match their exact needs. Sometimes it is extremely difficult, if not impossible, to find ways to present sensory and motor experiences that do match the child's needs.

These two forms of deprivation of sensory and motor experiences increase the risk of significant compromise in other areas of development. The MSE provides extensive opportunity for a wide range of carefully engineered and controlled sensory and motor experiences, thereby potentially aiding the ongoing development and/or maintenance of sensorimotor abilities. An important part of this literature therefore explores the relationship between the child's nervous system and the environment so more accurate matches of sensory and motor experiences with individual needs can be made.

To effectively plan and develop an IEP for a child with a disability (see Part III), the educator must not only have a broad understanding of how sensory and motor systems work in general, but also an insight into the particular sensory and motor problems being experienced by the child. The goal is more purposeful MSE use.

The sensorimotor system

Sensory and motor systems are interdependent and together form the sensori-motor system. The sensory system receives and transmits environmental stimuli, from the peripheral sense receptors to the spinal cord to the brain. There is neural integration at every level of the pathway, reshaping the transmitted information. The result is a complex constantly changing map of oneself (or body scheme) in relation to one's map of the environment. The body scheme is used to inform the motor system, to plan, organise and execute movement via the muscles. Sensory feedback from a motor response is used in turn to further enhance the body scheme.

An environmental stimulus activates a sensory system receptor to become a nervous system impulse. Receptors and nerves exhibit an all-or-none response; they are either activated (if the stimulus is of sufficient type and strength) or not. The level of stimulus just required to activate the receptor or nerve is called the stimulus threshold. It is the combination of the number and type of receptors that are activated that begins to characterise the stimulus perception. The receptors and nerves show some plasticity, in that the more they are used, the easier it tends to be to activate them (stimulus thresholds decrease). There is also plasticity with regard to the range of stimulus type that can activate a receptor. Previous experience and emotions have a complex effect and can profoundly modify stimulus thresholds, at every level but especially in the relays of the spinal cord and brain. Reflex arcs and perceived sensation are therefore to an extent context dependent. This accounts for why identical stimuli can result in different behaviours in different children, or even at different times in the same child.

Once the child's disability has been accurately assessed, it is possible to tune MSE stimuli so they fit within the child's particular stimulus thresholds and ranges. Conversely, modifying environmental stimuli can help with assessment. For example if a child with profound multiple disabilities responds to a visual stimulus in the MSE, this informs the observer the child can see in that particular situation at that particular time. It is important to avoid making generalisations based upon a single observation. Assessment must be conducted by different people, in different situations, at different times, using different measures to ensure that observations made are accurate and representative of the child's disability.

Within the sensory system there are six major sensory modalities where disability occurs. A sensation arouses and alerts the individual for each modality and provides information for discrimination of salient features of the stimuli. Alternatively stimuli may help to calm and relax the individual. Ease of movement along the arousal–relaxation continuum is a fundamental part of MSE design. For example with the sense of smell some aromas promote arousal (peppermint) while others promote relaxation (camomile). The same applies to each of the other senses (e.g. hearing and music). Other stimuli continua are high–low intensity, long–short time and wide–narrow range.

The somatosensory modality

The somatosensory modality consists of the senses of touch, pain, temperature, proprioception and balance. Touch matures early in humans and exerts a major influence on central nervous system development. Somatosensory receptors in the skin, especially those that relate to touch, pain and temperature inform the body scheme where the individual ends, the environment begins and the nature of the interface. Many early motor reflexes (e.g. rooting and grasping) are triggered through the somatosensory system. Important touch and temperature continua that are relevant to MSE design are hot–cold, rough–smooth and hard–soft.

Children with multiple disabilities who are unable to self-generate a sufficient volume of somatosensory information for environmental exploration rely heavily on carers to supply the deficit. The MSE makes it easy for the professional to create and maintain environmental opportunities for somatosensory exploration long beyond the time which would be required for non-disabled children. Awareness that some children with multiple disabilities experience ongoing problems with pain is important too.

Proprioception receptors are widespread in the joints, muscles and surrounding tissue. These proprioreceptors inform the body scheme of the relative whereabouts of movable body parts, and thus are extremely important for smooth integrated movement. Many natural exploratory activities of early childhood stimulate the proprioceptive system. Children with disabilities with high muscle tone may receive too much proprioceptive information, while children with low muscle tone may receive too little. These children therefore require a more specialised environment specifically designed to match their proprioceptive needs.

Head position and movement is detected by the vestibular system. The vestibular apparatus is located in the inner ear. Information from the vestibular apparatus is integrated with that from the eyes, body proprioreceptors and the body scheme to provide feedback to the motor system.

Organised, sequenced and well-timed body adjustments and movements result in balance.

Children with disabilities who experience difficulty moving independently are particularly reliant on adult intervention to structure the environment so that appropriate vestibular information is provided. Movements such as spinning and turning the child upside down help to stimulate arousal in the child, whereas rocking movements help to calm the child. The arousal–calming continuum is important for both proprioception and vestibular development.

Taste

Taste is the ability to recognise individual flavours through the taste buds (chemical receptors) in the mouth, especially on the tongue. The four basic taste qualities are bitterness, sweetness, sourness and saltiness. These come together in various combinations to form particular flavours. Taste is a strong motivator in the development of eating and drinking skills, such as sucking, chewing and swallowing. These activities encourage good muscle tone, a prerequisite for speech. Children with low oral muscle tone often have extremely limited experiences with tastes, mainly because of health risks such as the possibility of choking and inability to swallow. Such children are dependent upon carers to actively provide ongoing interesting taste experiences.

Smell

Smell is the ability to recognise individual odours through chemical receptors in the nose. The olfactory system can be moderately powerful. Babies from a very early age can identify their mother through smell (especially if she is breast feeding). Young children can identify each family member by their distinctive odours. Smells signal the familiar: people, places and objects. For a child with multiple disabilities, with impairment of a number of senses, the sense of smell may be particularly critical in helping to form a body scheme and to map the environment. Smell can be a crucial method for expanding the child's environmental experiences.

Hearing

Hearing is the ability to discriminate between sounds. Sound waves entering the outer ear canal are amplified by the ear drum and middle ear ossicles. They are then processed by the auditory receptors located in the cochlea in the inner ear. To identify the direction of sound, hearing can be coordinated with movement of the head and the vestibular system. Hearing is important in the development of speech. For children with hearing problems the environment needs to be acoustically sharp and devoid of background interference. Furthermore, providing increased opportunities for stimulation through the other senses, particularly visual, is also important.

Vision

The last sensory system to mature in the child is vision or the ability to see. The visual receptors are located in the retina, the light-sensitive inner lining of the eyeball. Different receptors react to different wavelengths of light. From the pattern of stimulation, cognitive perceptions of light and dark, form and colour are derived. These are in turn integrated into the body scheme and environmental map. Vision plays a primary role in every area of endeavour, especially movement and the use of objects. Visual system information is often integrated with that from other sensory systems. For example, hand–eye coordination involves somosensory, particularly touch and proprioception, and visual input.

In children with a visual impairment, opportunities need to be made available for stimulation through the other senses. As Fraiberg (1977) noted 'It is, of course, not blindness alone that closes the world for the child but insufficiency in the stimuli for tactile-kinesthetic-auditory function in the early years'.

The motor system

The infant is born with a range of automatic (reflex) and random movements. As the child grows, skills to organise and control movement develop. With practice these movements become more sophisticated and deliberate. Over time, a child learns to master complex movement skills, for example buttoning up a shirt, which requires sequencing of the component hand and arm movements.

Movement is often in response to sensory stimuli. Sensory, motor and cognitive systems are interlinked. Ongoing trial and error involving movement is a fundamental part of the learning process. Three purposes of movement are to restore equilibrium, to create a desired outcome (called motor planning or praxis) and to increase and refine skills.

Motivation for movement is important. It frequently comes from the environment, linked to cognition and past experience. It enables the individual to learn and perform ever more independent functional tasks related to daily life.

When the child has disabilities the environment may need ongoing modification in order to more closely meet the particular ongoing needs imposed by the disability. The MSE is well suited to these tasks. For example the ball pit may provide a child with increased opportunity to find a balance between stability and mobility thus enabling the child to move into positions of increased comfort.

Lilli Nielsen

Nielsen (1979; 1988; 1990a,b; 1991; 1992a,b; 1993a,b; 1994a,b) has done much to illuminate the nature of blindness and associated disabilities. In particular her research has focused on designing environments to motivate children with disabilities, especially visual impairment, to encourage exploration and experimentation. Over more than twenty years she has monitored 'active learning' processes, how the child with disabilities learns and develops in interaction with the environment. Nielsen's mission has been to increase opportunities for children with disabilities to develop to the best of their potential and to avoid unnecessarily delayed development.

Nielsen (1979) invited readers 'to think of the child's handicap as blindness *multiplied* by mental retardation' because 'the larger the number of handicaps, the greater is the risk that the child cannot make full use of the mental abilities he [or she] may possess' (p. 3). Nielsen argued that if blind children cannot find sufficiently challenging objects by themselves, and are 'not stimulated by being offered objects which challenge [utmost self-exertion] . . . development will be arrested . . . and . . . behaviour will likewise show signs of disturbances' (p. 37). In response to the child's need for challenging objects she created a 'treasure chest' consisting of a large number of everyday items including plastic plates, cups, brushes, tins, boxes, paper bags, balls and blocks.

She devised a comprehensive observation checklist of 27 areas to observe and record progress made by infants with visual impairment (Neilsen 1990a,b). It includes sight, behaviour of search without sight, development of spatial relations, development of the concept of quantity, development of temporal concept, gross and fine motor skills, communication, use of other senses, body awareness and daily living skills. Two further learning aids developed by Nielsen (1994b) are the 'essef board' and the 'resonance board'.

The essef board is a sprung board 'designed to facilitate the child's . . . learning to move his [her] legs, to help him [her] to achieve sufficient muscle strength and to encourage him [her] to learn to balance' (p. 23). The resonance board is a 2–3cm board that provides auditory feedback to movements made by the child. The child is able to kick against the essef board while lying on a resonance board, sit on the essef board or stand on it holding on to a support bar. A fourth learning aid, the 'little room' is also used with the resonance board.

Nielsen (1991) studied 20 congenitally blind infants (13 boys and 7 girls, aged 5 to 19 months) to determine whether the 'little room', a specially-designed 60 cm × 60 cm × 30 cm environment that fits over the child, would provide these infants with 'an early basis for developing awareness of spatial relations'. Results indicated that blindness was not a barrier to spatial cognitive development as long as 'infants are given an environment that enables them to achieve preunderstanding of the concept and permanence of objects and an awareness they can produce object based sounds' (p. 11). She concluded that

> While learning about spatial relations and the concept of permanence of objects, congenitally blind infants will rely on different cues from those that sighted infants depend on, but like sighted infants they need to

experience comparisons and engage in sequence games. However, such activities can be performed only if environments of sufficient quality are available to them. To be able to fulfil the blind infants' need for such environments, we professionals have to learn how blind infants experience their surroundings, how they integrate the sensory modalities, which materials motivate them to experiment and explore, how they transfer skills from one environment to another, and how they become contributors in interactions with others. Unless we understand the nature of blindness, congenitally blind infants may suffer from unnecessary delayed development. From observation and research, we must learn how to increase opportunities for blind infants to develop to the best of their potential. (p. 16)

Dunnett's (1997) case study of a four-and-a-half-year old blind girl Anna's use of the little room supported Nielsen's claims of its value (Nielsen 1992b). During her time in the little room Anna progressed through six of Nielsen's seven stages before being given the opportunity to play with Nielsen's 'treasure box'. The seven stages observed by Nielsen are:

1. accidental movements that resulted in the infants' gradual awareness of the objects hanging from the ceiling;
2. conscious pushing or touching of objects;
3. grasping and letting go, followed by grasping and keeping objects;
4. the immediate repetition of an activity;
5. varied handling of an object. Some of the infants became absorbed in tactile exploration and did not react to the sounds they produced concomitantly. Other infants started with integration of the kinesthetic and auditory senses. While exercising kinesthetic-auditory integration, they did not display tactile interest;
6. the infants listened at the same time as they performed a kinesthetic-tactile activity or began to perform a tactile search of the object with which a kinesthetic-auditory game was displayed;
7. the infants performed a quick search of one object while displaying a tactile search of another object; the aim clearly was to compare the tactile qualities of the two objects. The infants also performed different sounds with the same object or with two objects to compare the sounds. In addition they quickly grasped several objects one after another as if to compare the position of the objects or to assure themelves of the presence of the objects. In this stage the infants began to play games that involved a sequence of specific actions. (Nielsen 1991, pp. 13–14)

A number of authors have described the MSE as an extension of Nielsen's little room (Hepworth 1993; Melberg and Jansson 1994; Bozic and Murdoch 1994; Hirstwood and Gray 1995; Mount and Cavet 1995; Pagliano 1997a). The ramifications are fascinating.

A. Jean Ayres

A second author often cited in the literature is A. Jean Ayres, an occupational therapist who worked with children who had perceptual, learning and behaviour problems of unidentified origin. Ayres (1979) developed an influential 'sensory integration theory' to explain the relationship between sensory processing and behaviour. The primary objective of her theory was to explain the underlying causes of sensorimotor learning problems and thereby determine appropriate treatment methods. Ayres (1989) described sensory integration as

> the neurological process that organizes sensation from one's own body and from the environment and makes it possible to use the body effectively within the environment. The spatial and temporal aspects of inputs from different sensory modalities are interpreted, associated, and unified. Sensory integration is information processing . . . . The brain must select, enhance, inhibit, compare, and associate the sensory information in a flexible, constantly changing pattern; in other words, the brain must integrate it. (p. 11)

The theory was based on five variably contentious assumptions: neural plasticity, developmental sequence, nervous system hierarchy, adaptive behaviour and inner drive. There are three interrelated facets: theory, evaluation methods and treatment techniques. Sensory integration theory was developed from detailed study of young children with mild to moderate learning difficulties who had no discernible sensory impairments. Generalising to a wider population, including children with sensory impairments, is opportunistic.

From the theory came 'sensory integrative therapy', an influential development of relevance to the MSE.

> The central idea of this therapy is to provide and control sensory input, especially the input from the vestibular system, muscles and joints, and skin in such a way that the child spontaneously forms the adaptive responses that integrate those sensations. (Ayres 1979, p. 140)

Sensory stimuli used included brushing or rubbing the skin, deep pressure, vibration, smell and vestibular arousal. Equipment commonly used included the scooter board and bolster swing. 'If the environment is optimal for . . . [a] child's growth, he [she] will feel that therapy is "fun" . . . . The therapist tries to balance structure and freedom in a way that leads to constructive exploration' (p. 151). The therapist 'requires a great deal of training, imagination and sensitivity' (p. 147).

Ayres has been criticised for circularity and lack of clarity in some of her work; the theory is deceptively simple. Often therapy, nominally sensory integrative, has strayed beyond the boundaries of the theory. Fisher and Murray

(1991) proposed a new conceptual model of sensory integration to try to deal with these criticisms

> the spiral process of self-actualization ... Sub-spirals or feedback loops ... allow the open system to regulate and organise itself ... An important component of this model is the inclusion of behavioural as well as neuro-biological components. (p. 18)

The authors advise that 'critical analysis of sensory integration theory and practice should remain an ongoing process .... Theory is provisional' (p. 24).

Play

The MSE is often cited as a supportive environment for the development of play skills. Bundy (1991) defined play as

> a transaction between an individual and the environment that is intrinsically motivated, internally controlled, and free of many of the constraints of objective reality ... play transactions are considered to represent a continuum of behaviors that are more or less playful, depending on the degree to which the criteria are present. (p. 59)

This means that the play–non-play continuum is determined by the interplay between three further continua, namely: external–internal control, extrinsic–intrinsic motivation, objective reality–suspension of reality.

This definition of play enables the professional to work towards the development of play skills through intervention. For example, Skellenger and Hill (1994) studied 'the effects of a shared teacher–child play intervention to increase the amount and type of targeted play behavior of three young children who are blind' (p. 433). This involved the use of non-directive strategies, including following the child's lead, modelling and participation as a play partner. All three children showed improvements in their play behaviour after the intervention.

Rubin et al. (1983) identified five design features to help make an environment more conducive to play. They are:

1. an array of familiar peers, toys, or other materials likely to engage children's interest;
2. an agreement between adults and children, expressed in word, gesture, or established by convention, that the children are free to choose from the array whatever they wish to do within whatever limits are required by the setting or the study;
3. adult behavior that is minimally intrusive or directive;
4. a friendly atmosphere designed to make children feel comfortable and safe; and

5. scheduling that reduces the likelihood of the children being tired, hungry, ill, or experiencing other types of bodily stress. (p. 701)

Of course, some features must be specially designed to match individual sense needs. Schneekloth (1989) conducted research where she compared the motor and environmental interactions of sighted and children with visual impairment. She concluded that some developmental delays in children with visual impairment are the result of 'lack of opportunity for gross motor inter-actions' (p. 196). She recommended

> that intervention programs with two foci be established for children with visual impairments. First, there is a need for appropriately designed environments that are *accessible, safe, exciting,* and *complex.* Second, training programs should be established for service providers which facilitate the development of environmental competence, i.e. the use of the environment as an active tool in achieving the educational objectives for each child. (p. 201)

Tröster and Brambring (1994) argued that 'blind children's acquisition of individual types of play behavior . . . take a different course' from sighted children. They recommended

> For functional play with objects, it is necessary to develop play materials that elicit an interesting tactile or auditory effect when manipulated, such as building blocks that play ascending notes on a musical scale when they are placed on top of each other in the correct order. Only specifically designed play materials that allow blind children to have manual control over the cause and effect of their actions and motivate the children by the auditory or tactile effect they elicit will stimulate the children to play with objects. (p. 430)

Rettig (1994) defined six types of play in ascending order of complexity. They are:

1. solitary play where the child is unaware of other children;
2. parallel play where the child plays near, but not with, another child;
3. functional–manipulative play where the child uses a plaything in the way it was intended;
4. symbolic play where two children agree that an object is something else;
5. dramatic play where a child is engaged in pretend role-play; and
6. cooperative play where children play together and there is give and take.

The use of specifically designed switches that allow children to have manual control over the cause and effect of their actions will be explored in Chapter 4.

Explicit value base

O'Brien's (1987) 'five accomplishments' were identified by Hirstwood and Gray (1995) as the most widely-used guide to interpreting the principles of normalisation and social role valorisation (Wolfensberger 1972; 1984) when using the MSE. These five accomplishments encourage professionals to consider the social and emotional environment as well as the physical environment. They are:

1. choice, perhaps the most important principle of MSE use; choice requires communication and some level of self-advocacy, and helps the child own the learning and is necessary for play to occur;
2. community participation. This refers to the right of the individual with a disability to access the community, particularly the same leisure facilities as those used by the non-disabled population. The MSE can be such an option in a repertoire of possible leisure experiences;
3. respect, highlighting the importance of individuals with disabilities being consistently treated with dignity. This necessitates that throughout the MSE experience (including going to, attending and leaving) the individual's wishes are acknowledged and that attention is given to ensuring that the individual is feeling safe, secure and comfortable;
4. relationships; each individual needs to have culturally valued relationships beyond that of the professional. If the MSE is a multifunctional environment where non-disabled people as well as those with disabilities are welcome, then there will be appropriate opportunities for the development of culturally valued relationships;
5. competence, largely determined by a self-fulfilling prophesy that individuals either live up or down to the expectations of others. If there are high expectations for individuals when they use the MSE, they are more likely to achieve greater success than if there are low expectations.

These accomplishments were later extended to include (O'Brien 1990):

6. continuity;
7. individuality.

The model focuses heavily on the individual. It is important that educators take a holistic view and see their students as embedded in the family, within the wider community.

Conclusion

These ideas lay the basis for subsequent chapters. It is important to be rigorous to differentiate between speculation, theory and fact, a goal that the academic MSE literature has poorly achieved to date. Each child with a disability has his or her own perception of reality and this is the starting point for MSE design and use.

Table 3.1 Continua identified in Chapter 3

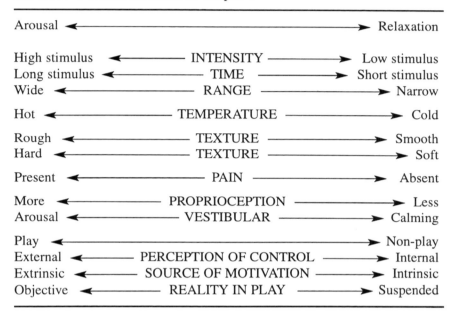

PART II:
Design and construction

Chapter 4

What facilities could be included in the MSE?

Introduction

Decisions regarding what to include in the MSE should be primarily shaped by the needs of individual child users. The MSE only has value as an educational tool if it is meaningful to the child in positive ways (see Chapter 1). In this chapter, a wide range of items that could be included in a MSE is introduced and possible uses outlined. These uses will then be further developed in subsequent chapters, especially those relating to curriculum.

General considerations

The physical nature of a MSE is determined by the needs of the user and the intelligence and sensitivity of the staff that manage it, ideally a transdisciplinary team because of its integrated approach (see Chapter 5). The staff need to consider a variety of aspects when purchasing equipment, such as cost, value for money, durability, safety, storability (see Chapter 7). It is of course not possible to exhaustively catalogue all the items that could possibly be included in a MSE, for the list is endless.

Kewin (1991c) argued that 'more equipment does not mean more success'. Too many items can cause clutter and can even be counter-productive. Each item present in the MSE should be justified both by its intrinsic value and also by its concordant relationship to the other equipment.

Likewise, more expensive does not mean more success. Many benefits accrue from the use of cheap, simple, home-made items. Such items can be quickly 'tailor-made' to suit specific needs. If items are disappointing, not fulfilling their anticipated potential, they can be discarded without undue budgetary regret. Being less precious, the staff have more freedom to experiment. If items are broken they can easily be repaired or reconceptualised. The commonplace nature of the materials used has an additional benefit of involving parents, friends and community in MSE design, development and production. This results in increased levels of ongoing interest in how the environment is being used, promoting better links between the home and the

MSE. Involvement of children from mainstream schools in design problem solving can also be fruitful.

In my experience the more expensively-stocked MSEs do tend to be less flexible in their range of uses. This may well be because they have been designed and constructed by individuals who work for a commercial company. Ideally the MSE needs to be designed collaboratively by all the members of a transdisciplinary team of professionals, parents and interested friends who will be directly involved in using the MSE (see Chapter 5). Collectively these stakeholders are in a position to respond to the needs of the individual child users. When an outside expert from a commercial company designs and constructs the MSE there is naturally an external locus of control.

This does not mean to say that commercial items are without value. On the contrary, there are many excellent commercial products available. Commercial catalogues are a useful source of new ideas (ROMPA, TFH, Mike Ayres Design, Spacekraft, Royal National Institute for the Blind (RNIB). Similarly, when designing a MSE, I recommend visiting as many up and running MSEs as possible. The more extensive the preparation, the better the final design is likely to be.

Room types

A fundamental aspect of design relevant to all room types is size. The size of the room is an important dictate of the number and type of items that can be included; as suggested above, often simplicity is best. However one large room can contain several smaller rooms, constructed using movable partitions.

In line with current understanding of cognitive development, it would seem advisable to match this smaller room size with the size of the child's world, that is the size of the world of which the child shows awareness (see Chapter 3). When children are first born their world is very immediate. They respond to primary sensations that are within their sphere of influence (approximately 15 cm for vision). This sphere of influence gradually increases as the child grows and acquires new skills – as his or her body scheme expands.

The assumption is that if the room is matched to the child's world size, then the child will feel more in control of the environment. Hopkins *et al.* (1994) supported this assumption when they concluded

> Sensory environments are credited with miraculous powers but it turns out that the striking effects that a child and his [her] carer experience are brought about because they are in a small enough secluded space for the child to be able to conceptualise the whole space and the persons within it. Every other room in the school or centre might be beyond the child's capacity to appreciate – too big, too complicated, too many people. This room replicates the effects staff have noticed when unresponsive children

are taken on caravan holidays. Suddenly they realise where they are and that the scale is manageable. They can begin to signal and expect their communications to be received. Lilli Nielsen's Little Room is the clearest example of reducing the world to an appropriate scale. (pp. 2–3)

The greater the disparity between room size and child's sphere of influence, the more likely it is that the child will be overwhelmed. This is also the case regarding complexity. Over a period of time the room size and complexity can be expanded, evolving with the child as new needs emerge.

For children with severe physical disabilities careful consideration must be given to both location and positioning. The child needs to be placed in locations that are interesting and meaningful to the child. This could be in a beanbag under a fibre-optic spray, in the ball pool or beside the bubble tube. Objects must be stable, restricted in movement to ensure they remain within the child's movement range and have been adapted to fit the individual child's needs (e.g. switches designed to match child's movement skills, Velcro straps on child and object to support grasping). Positioning refers to how the child is physically arranged in that location. Good positioning utilises sound ergodynamic principles to promote comfort and physical well-being while optimising opportunities for observation and providing maximum freedom for controlled yet relaxed movement. The occupational therapist and physiotherapist will help determine the special location and positioning needs of individual children (see Chapter 5). Careful attention must also be given to deciding when it is best to change positioning and/or location.

Other considerations, apart from size and complexity, include the provision of a store cupboard for items not currently in use, good quiet ventilation and appropriate heating and cooling. MSEs have been categorised into a number of different room types, each associated with particular uses – each with their own historical development.

White room

The white room originated in The Netherlands with Hulsegge and Verheul (1986/7) and is currently the most popular MSE in use. The white room is often used for leisure, relaxation, aromatherapy and massage. Because it was originally designed for adults, the space has tended to be large. There are however examples of small white rooms developed specifically for children in early childhood.

The white walls, floor, ceiling and furnishings become one large three-dimensional screen for the projection of coloured effects and other lighting displays including mirror balls and pin spots. The white room is therefore designed to provide maximum contrast between visual figure and ground, the figures being the equipment and visual effects and the ground being the white surfaces. Equipment housed in the white room can include bubble tubes, soft play matting and constructions, a ball pool and fibre optics.

Although white when the lights are on, when the lights are switched off, having no windows, the room becomes pitch black. The room is usually kept in semi-darkness with soft, soothing music playing in the background.

> The lack of colour in the decor of the 'White Room' may be seen as offering very little stimulation in itself and the attention can then be on the activity carried out, rather than being distracted by bright coloured furniture and hard uncomfortable floors. The room will have its own identification for some people and may be the only area where a person is not confused by too much stimulus and understands that they are in an area where there are less demands and less pressure placed upon them to achieve. (Hirstwood and Gray 1995, p. 22)

Hirstwood and Gray (1995) caution that the lack of colour contrasts could make the room seem quite threatening and disorientating, especially for someone with a visual impairment entering the room for the first time. The first visit could also be difficult for a child with autism; careful attention must therefore be given to the introductory visit; each child needs to be introduced to the MSE in a way that suits that particular child. The educator should identify potential problems and develop strategies to assist the individual to overcome these problems. For example if the problem is visual, the visitor could first be taken to a room with a white carpet to see if this creates any problems. If the visitor is autistic there may need to be many visits before the child is invited to move into the room and participate. Common sense suggestions include: watch the MSE on video, visit the MSE when it is empty, introduce the room gradually, point out salient features (such as floor, walls, ceiling, exit and displays), allow the visitor time to explore the room before dimming the house lights, begin with only one display. If the visitor still feels uncomfortable he or she may like to be seated near the entrance with the door wide open.

Dark room

Dark rooms were originally developed by professionals working with children with visual impairment, particularly in the area of visual assessment, stimulation and 'training' (Reed 1992). The room can vary in size, from a small converted cupboard to a classroom (Longhorn 1988; Lister 1993). Walls, ceiling and floor are painted black. Like the white room, when the lights are switched off, the room is in complete darkness.

Hirstwood and Gray (1995) reasoned that the room was painted black because 'black soaks light in ... offers very little reflection and glare [furthermore] ... brighter and more defined areas of light can be created ... so offering a better room for studying visual awareness' (pp. 22–3). Equipment used in the room includes torches, fibre optics, iridescent shapes, coloured lights, ultravoilet lighting and dimmers (Best 1992). Often the dark room houses similar equipment to that found in the white room.

Like the white room, the dark room provides a neutral ground which helps to highlight the equipment and effects. The contrasts against a black ground are heightened, more powerful than against a white ground. One method to further intensify visual image is through fluorescence. Diffey (1993) described fluorescence as

> When certain materials are exposed to ultraviolet radiation the molecules present in the material can absorb the ultraviolet rays and re-emit radiation of a longer wavelength – normally visible light. This is particularly striking in materials to which *optical brighteners* are added such as paper, detergents and fabrics. Optical brighteners are compounds which absorb radiation in the 320–400 nm region (UVA) and emit light, or *fluoresce*, in the 400–500 nm region of the visible light spectrum which corresponds to blue light. (p. 11)

It is important to be aware that, like a white room, to a child with a disability a dark room may seem just as threatening or disorientating.

Sound room

Sound rooms were originally developed by professionals working with children with hearing impairment, particularly in the area of auditory assessment, auditory stimulation, auditory 'training' (Luetke-Stahlman and Luckner 1991, p. 201), music and speech work. The room can vary in size, from that of a store cupboard to a classroom. Room construction usually involves lining the walls and ceiling with acoustically sensitive material and having a sprung wooden floor.

When the doors are closed, the room should be cut off from all outside noises, including those produced by air conditioners and electrical equipment. There needs to be maximum contrast between the neutral auditory ground and auditory figures. Further amplification can be achieved through the use of echo chambers, resonance boards and FM transmitters linked to hearing aids.

It is also possible to make the room acoustically dull by using sound absorbers. This can be achieved by padding the walls with corrugated cardboard, egg cartons or cork tiles, by hanging curtains, covering the floor with carpets and hanging soft materials from the ceiling.

Interactive room

In the interactive room the focus is on providing increased opportunities for the child to understand the relationship between cause and effect. Interaction is achieved through the use of specially designed switches or movement sensitive equipment. Addis (not dated) defined a switch as 'Any gadget which allows . . . [an individual] by a very small movement of her [his] body, to produce an effect which she [he] finds pleasing or rewarding' (p. 5).

Reed and Addis (1996) argue that interaction

> ... may be achieved by analyzing what we describe as 'strategies of empowerment'. ... we employ switching systems to pass the locus of control over to a child. Switching systems lend themselves to this aim. ... We want to capitalize upon an arrangement whereby, with a small movement of some part of his or her body, the child can produce a grand rewarding effect. We are prepared to use anything if we are sure that the child enjoys, or is proud of his or her actions. ... For one little boy, who has limited arm movement and some vision, we stack up a pile of cardboard boxes, painted in bright colours, next to his chair. He squeals with delight when a tiny push sends them crashing down. (p. 93)

Equipment which has been designed to promote interaction include the soundbeam, sound light floors, interactive infinity tunnels, lights and fans.

Water room

Water is perhaps the most under-utilised natural resource in sensory education. Hulsegge and Verheul (1986/7) argued that 'water has abundant possibilities, it wraps around your body and feels comfortable and warm when it is properly heated' (p. 102). Water supports body weight and makes it easier to move. Water can be used to explore the relationship between cause and effect. Hulsegge and Verheul (1986/7) aimed to create a tropical environment in their water room, by screening off the pool windows and by adding dimmers and underwater lighting as well as numerous plastic plants. Another water room with a large jacuzzi pool was described by Hutchinson and Haggar (1991) as part of the Whittington Hall Project.

A third water room was described by Rotherham (1996). This room at Mill House School was purpose-built for students with multiple disabilities. It consists of

> ... a trough for general water exploration, showers of varying intensities ranging from gentle wash to needlepoint spray, an adjustable jacuzzi/whirlpool, and a waterfall which students can experience by sitting in front of, under or behind .... Lights of different colours are positioned to reflect off and through the water, to aid development of visual awareness and as a specific teaching aid for those who respond to a particular colour. Finally, our aquatherapy room offers what is perhaps the most important element of all – that of student control. The jacuzzi, showers, lights and waterfall are all controlled by simple infra-red switches, which enable students to switch the effects on and off simply by moving their hand, foot, or other body part, across the front of the switch. (p. 22)

Rotherham described the water room as 'an important new vehicle for sensory education' because it offers an appropriate level of stimulation for individual users (p. 23). She identified showers, waterfall and lights as generally stimulating and the jacuzzi as more relaxing.

For Hirstwood and Gray (1995) the downside of the water room is that it is expensive to build and maintain; moisture is harsh on most equipment. Individuals with disabilities using the environment require close supervision. Furthermore the environment needs to be kept at a suitable temperature for its users and particular emphasis placed on ensuring that hygiene and safety measures are strictly followed (see Chapter 7 for discussion on health and safety issues).

Soft play room

The soft play environment may include ball pools, soft play furnishings and/or hard plastic shapes that can be used for building, climbing, running, jumping, bouncing, rolling or sliding. They are particularly popular with young children who enjoy manipulating the solid shapes to construct new spaces of their own – a cubby hole or a secret cave. Soft play environments work well for children with visual impairment who might be inhibited when playing in playgrounds. Soft play environments also work well for children with physical disabilities who find movement difficult and are used for relief of stress in children who are hyperactive or autistic. Soft play environments provide a safe place where children can let off steam. They offer a positive means of creating security for some children.

Verandah, garden and other locations

The MSE need not be confined to a room. It is possible to design an environment on a verandah, a hallway, a tent or even outside in the garden. Walls and Dayan (1992) explained how outdoor sound sculptures could be built from scrap materials. Reed and Addis (1994) described a series of interactive workboards which were developed to line a corridor outside a school classroom. Mount (1993) reported on the building of a multisensory garden in an open quadrangle, while Manor (1994) told of the involvement of a group of architecture students in designing a multisensory adventure playground.

MSE designs

The range of possible MSE designs is limited only be the imagination, expertise and resources of the designers. As Hirstwood and Gray (1995) surmise

> For some people white may be too clinical, black may be too threatening, soft play rooms too exciting and theme rooms too complex to create. Possibly a hybrid of all the rooms is the type you will choose if you are not

going to be fixed to one philosophy. One or two floor mats in the room, rather than a whole floor, coloured white on one side and black on the other may help the floor problem. This way you can project on to the white side or use the black side to create bright contrasts when using fibre optics and other equipment. We are in favour of giving people control over the environment so that switching systems can play an important part. The walls may be a light not white colour; you could have a curtain around the room .... Don't just think about what looks nice, think about the implications for the children ... (pp. 33–4)

Their idea of a hybrid MSE corresponds with the 'open-minded space' concept (see Chapter 2). The wider the MSE remit the greater the range of dimensions that can be explored to identify successful stimulus matches for particular children. Combining dimensions often requires considerable creative ingenuity.

What to include?

This section lists equipment items that could be included in a MSE (see Table 4.1).

This is by no means an exhaustive list; it does not include every single commercial item. It does not include all the types of items that have been 'tailor made' for an individual child. Journals such as *Information Exchange* and *Eye Contact* are useful resources for the MSE design team in this regard. For example, Edwards (1992) describes how to make a tactile board from everyday junk materials. Sharing experience, an important aspect of MSE design and usage, will be further developed in Chapter 11.

Two particular therapeutic modalities often used in the MSE, mentioned in the table above but needing further elaboration, are aromatherapy and massage.

Aromatherapy

Aromatherapy is a holistic, complementary therapy involving the use of essential oils. ('Holistic' means that the treatment takes into account the person's lifestyle, emotional state and stress factors. 'Complementary' means that it can be used in conjunction with other approaches, including conventional medicine.) The strength of aromatherapy is that it is comparatively simple, easy to administer and is based on the use of natural minimally invasive ingredients and techniques. The individual receiving the therapy can remain passive or choose to interact.

Table 4.1 Items that could be included in a MSE

Item	Brief description	Possible uses
General lighting with dimmers	Natural lighting for the space needed for cleaning and setting up equipment	To aid movement within MSE. Relaxation
Sound system	CD, cassette player, radio Power connections required. Portable	For background music, sound effects, stories. Relaxation
Television set and VCR effects	Power connections required. Could be portable	For visual/sound/dramatic. Relaxation
Mirror ball Pin spot Rotator (drive unit) Sparkle ball (alternative)	Diameter 20 or 30 cm. Spotlight shone onto slowly rotating mirror ball to cast myriad of moving light reflections. Power connections for drive and spot	Creates interesting visual effects. Atmosphere. If located on ceiling, lights entire space
Solar 250 projector Wheel rotator Prism/kaleidoscope lens Variety of wheel effects	Slowly-moving fluid patterns or special images are thrown onto the walls, floor and ceiling. Power connections required	Creates interesting visual effects. Atmosphere. If located on ceiling, lights entire space. Can be focused on one wall
Crystal pulse Amplifier box and microphone	Attached to solar 250 projector and to sound source. Power connections required	Visual reward when sounds are made
Spotlight and colour wheel	Constantly rotating sparkles of light. Unit gets hot, so attach to ceiling. Power connections required	Visually stimulating, tracking
Ultraviolet effects (UV type A light) Fluorescent hoops, rods, paint, markers, balls, earth, moon, galaxy Linelite plastic tubing, magic wands	For use in dark room. Effects depend upon UV lamp. Effects use normal white light. (See Chapter 7 for safety guidelines)	Highly stimulating visually. Visual exploration. Draw pictures. Write 'glow in the dark' messages
Fibre optics, fountain tails, waterfall, curtain, spray, travelling light tube, picture maker, fibre-optic torch/lamp Light source	Glass fibre encased in a silicone rubber or PVC sheath to give protection and flexibility. Light from source extends along the length of the fibre. Fixed or mobile. Power connections required for light source	Light can be touched, moved, explored, manipulated. Changing colours encourage focus of attention. Decoration or cool lighting
Plasma ball	A glass globe that responds to either sound or hand contact to produce visual effect. Power connection required	Tactile, visual, auditory cause and effect. Suitable for withdrawn user

Table 4.1 *continued*

Item	Brief description	Possible uses
Sound and light floor, wall, hopscotch, sound effects units, micro-phones sound-sensitive toys	Sound-activated visual displays. Weight-activated visual and sound displays. Sound-activated visually organised response (e.g. louder for higher). Power connections required	Tactile, visual and auditory cause and effect
Soundbeam Midisynthesiser Midicreator (similar to soundbeam but less sensitive). Midigesture, midisensor	Consists of a control box and transducer. A beam bounces back from an object (e.g. hand). The transducer emits an electronic pulse to a particular note or chord – if object moves closer, note becomes higher MIDI (Musical Instrument Digital Interface)	If range is very short, slightest movement will produce sound changes – suit immobile child. Movement with auditory reward. Movement and auditory cause and effect
Bubble tube Bubble wall Bubble column mirrors Passive/interactive	Diameter 15 or 30cm. Length 1 to 1.75m. Boiled/distilled water, change regularly. Bubble speed slow to fast. Switch to control coloured lights or automatic slow colour changes	Visual effect produced by rising bubbles and lighting plus sounds. Gentle vibration makes pleasing tactile effect. Combined visual, auditory and tactile experience.
Switches Touch pads, large, small feet, hands, squeeze lever Collar switch Activity-complete switch Remote control	operated by hand/feet or body movement operated by movements of the head operated when activity correctly completed	User control. Self determination. Cause and effect. Perseverence.
Aromatherapy diffuser, aroma fan, interactive aroma box, essential oils, and massage oils (see next section)	Pomanders, scented cushions, smell box, incense, essential oils. Power connection required	Aromatherapy and massage for relaxation and stimulation. Stimulates the olfactory and somatosensory systems
Hydrotherapy jacuzzi/whirlpool, trough, bath, shower, waterfall, fountain	Full range of water equipment. Water treatment necessary. Water safety requirements. Power connection required for heating.	Hydrotherapy. Water play. Movement. Stimulation/relaxation.
Wind chimes Mobiles	Wind chimes of any shape or size. Mobiles of any shape or size.	Auditory stimulation, relaxation. Visual stimulation, relaxation.
Water beds	Variety of sizes, types, colours and prices. Power point for water heater. Strong floor support required.	Adjusts to body weight. For comfort and relaxation
Ball pools	Variety of sizes, shapes and prices. Balls clear, white, single or multicoloured. Ball size (diameter 6 to 7.5 cm). Net for washing balls	Small balls suit young child. Large balls suit active use. Provide safety, body support. Clear balls for illumination.

Table 4.1 *continued*

Item	Brief description	Possible uses
Beanbags	Variety of sizes, shapes, colours and prices	Sitting, lying, relaxation
Air cushion/mattress	Variety of sizes, shapes, colours and prices	Sitting, lying, relaxation
Vibrating cushion, pillow, mattress	Variety of sizes, shapes, colours and prices. Vibrates when pressure applied	Sitting, lying, relaxation. Tactile cause and effect
Music – CDs, cassettes sound effects musical instruments	Classical, popular, New Age. Animals, nature, waterfall, ocean. Instruments that produce musical sounds	Relaxation or stimulation Relaxation or stimulation Interaction
Soft play floor, walls, ceiling, cushioning, solid shapes – triangle, semi-circle, circle, rectangle, square	Nylon re-inforced flame retardant PVC filled with fire resistant foam to make a wide range of cushions and shapes. Velcro strips for linking units together	For movement activities. Relaxation and leisure. Construction, manipulation, experimentation. Social play
Tactile panels, wall, features, carpets, hangings	Different textures to provide a variety of tactile sensations. Can be made out of household items such as broom and mop heads, brushes, plastic plates, string, wool	Tactile stimulation. Tactile exploration

Sanderson and Ruddle (1992) identified six goals of aromatherapy. They are to:

1. facilitate relaxation and reduce stress
2. invigorate and promote activity and alertness
3. stimulate sensory awareness
4. facilitate and encourage interaction and communication
5. treat medical problems using natural substances
6. provide natural pain relief. (p. 311)

Wild (1996) added three further goals when using aromatherapy with individuals with disabilities, that of increasing body awareness, increasing toleration of physical contact and recognition of choice.

Essential oils are essences obtained from different parts of fragrant plants (flowers, seeds, leaves, bark, wood, root or whole plant) using a range of extraction methods from steam distillation to pressing. Essential oils are volatile, that is they are easily vaporised. The three main ways of using essential oils in aromatherapy are: diluted in a carrier oil for masage, diluted in water for bathing or vaporised into the air through a burner. Three less-often used methods are compresses, creams and inhalations.

A carrier oil is an unscented vegetable oil (grapeseed, sweet almond). Usually five percent wheatgerm oil is added to help preserve the carrier oil.

Sanderson (1995) recommended blending two drops of essential oil per 5 ml (one teaspoon) of carrier oil. Essential oils can be used singularly or in combination. Once the mixture is shaken it is ready for use in massage (see below).

Essential oils can be diluted in bath water of an appropriate temperature, adding up to six drops (consisting of one, two or three different scents). Essential oil can also be placed in a foot bath.

There are a number of different burners available for vaporising the essential oil into the ambient air. The traditional burner is either ceramic or brass, housing a candle to heat a shallow bowl containing up to 12 drops of essential oil diluted in water. This method is not recommended for use in MSEs, being potentially dangerous because it involves the use of a naked flame and hot water. Another method is to use an electric diffuser to heat the diluted essential oil, but the diffuser must be placed safely out of reach of exploring hands. A third, and probably the safest, method involves the use of a vaporising ring. The vaporising ring fits onto a lightbulb and when the lightbulb is switched on, the aroma permeates the room.

Essential oils themselves are basically safe, provided they are not applied undiluted directly to the skin or taken by mouth. However it is important to be aware of the possibility of allergy, which can be severe. Diffey (1993) specifically cautions against using bergamot oil under UV light. He explains that bergamot oil

> contains the chemical 5-methoxypsoralen which is a potent photosensitising agent. When skin to which bergamot oil has been applied is exposed to UVA radiation, a phototoxic reaction can occur resulting in reddening and persistent pigmentation. It is sensible, therefore, not to use ultraviolet blacklight lamps for visual stimulation if bergamot oil has been applied to the skin in the previous 24 hours. (p. 11)

More than 50 essential oils are readily available for purchase commercially. Each oil is thought to have special therapeutic qualities, the range includes being:

- antiseptic
- antifungal
- anti-inflammatory
- antidepressant
- decongestant
- sedative
- relaxing
- stimulating.

The usual use of aromatherapy in the MSE is to help the user relax. Oils with relaxing, soothing, calming properties include:

- camomile
- eucalyptus

- frankincense
- jasmine
- lavender
- rose and
- ylang-ylang.

Oils with stimulatory, invigorating, arousing properties include:

- basil,
- cinnamon
- clary sage
- lemon
- patchouli
- peppermint and
- rosemary.

However, different people react in different ways to different aromas. For this reason group aromatherapy in the MSE can be counter-productive. It is important to keep a record of negative as well as positive experiences to various scents, to build up a profile of the child's preferences. Emphasis when using essential oils with children with disabilities must be placed on choice by the child and sensitivity of the educator.

Massage

Massage has many uses, within a variety of disciplines. Generally it is a remedial treatment involving stroking, kneading, rubbing, applying pressure and otherwise manipulating a part or the whole of the body. Massage can be self-administered or conducted by a second person, with or without lotions or oils. There are many different methods of massage: Swedish, shiatsu, acupressure, to name only a few (Westland 1993a,b).

Massage can confer several physical benefits. It can:

- help relieve muscle aches and pains, cramps and joint stiffness;
- be relaxing, reducing stress and anxiety;
- improve blood circulation, promote good posture, improve breathing and aid chest physiotherapy;
- help overcome problems of constipation;
- help reduce muscle tone when hands, feet or other parts of the body become locked in spasms.

Conversely, it can help:

- increase muscle tone when tone is low and so reduce muscle wastage in people who are paralysed;
- prevent abnormal growth in children with severe physical disabilities;
- prevent bed sores in those who are confined to bed.

Massage can also confer psychological benefits. It can make a person feel emotionally reassured and comforted. Rich (1990) argued that the positive effects of touch therapy in society are wide ranging.

> Although you can't kill someone with kindness, lack of affection can be fatal. . . . Touch therapy is now regarded as important in all areas – patients in hospitals recover more quickly from surgery, the handicapped learn faster, and the emotionally disturbed respond to psychiatric treatment more positively. (p. 10)

Two types of massage commonly used in the MSE for relaxation are hand and foot massage (see Box 4.1) using either hand cream or massage oil.

Rich (1996) listed seven basic massage movements: stroking, raking, pummelling, friction rub, thumbing and kneading. It is important that the educator consult with the physiotherapist regarding which massage movements are suitable. Some children have very fragile bones and may only be able to have very gentle stroking.

Hand massage

1. Add cream or oil by gently playing with your partner's hand.
2. Stretch the palms out widthways, then gently push the fingers backwards.
3. Push the knuckles downwards.
4. Rub the hand vigorously with friction strokes between your own hands.
5. Gently pull and twist each finger and the thumb from base to tip.
6. Using your thumbs only, gently massage in small circles around the wrist.
7. Using your thumbs and fingers, gently knead and fan stroke all the tiny bones from the fingertips to wrist.
8. Sandwich the hand between your palms at the wrist and pull towards you in a slow, long stroke, ending with the fingertips.
9. Repeat for other hand.

Foot massage

1. Gently play with partner's foot while applying cream or oil.
2. Sandwich foot between the palms of your hands and stroke firmly from toes to ankles.
3. Vigorously rub heel with your palms for two minutes to stimulate blood flow and warm the foot.
4. Hold and wiggle toes.
5. Gently pull each toe from base to tip.
6. Push under arch with your knuckles.
7. Knead the entire sole from ball to heel.
8. Massage all around the ankle, making small circles with your thumbs.
9. Twist and wring the foot.
10. Sandwich foot between your palms, stroking slowly and firmly from ankle to toes several times.
11. Repeat for other foot.

Box 4.1 Hand and foot massage

A group massage technique called 'atmospherics' was devised by Laurent (1992) where 'Large semi-transparent silks are sensitively drawn over the heads and bodies of the group in rotation' (p. 19). Massage can also play an important role in the MSE in regard to the child's emotional and social development. Pagliano (1997a) reported these illustrative comments.

> In the . . . [MSE] the children will turn to each other. This is something that they don't do in their classroom. In the . . . [MSE] they actually reach out for each other. If one child is having a massage on the arms then another child is watching, being part of the experience. Not only are the children becoming more aware, I think a sort of friendship is developing. (Teacher)

Conclusion

A goal of this book is to provide stakeholders with sufficient information, to enable them to make informed decisions regarding how to design their MSE and what equipment to include. Of primary importance are the needs of individual users.

These needs are identified through the ongoing observation, evaluation and assessment of the child by members of staff. The best design will emerge from the ongoing collaborative involvement of a transdisciplinary team involving teachers and teacher's aides, occupational therapists, physiotherapists, communication therapists, parents and family. Undoubtedly each team member will bring to the design different priorities and assumptions which will need to be coordinated and incorporated into the overall MSE. The end result is a multifunctional integrated 'open-minded' space. Just how this transdisciplinary approach can be achieved is the subject of the next chapter.

Table 4.2 Continua identified in Chapter 4

Large ◄───────────	ROOM SIZE ──────────►	Small
White ◄───────────	ROOM COLOUR ─────────►	Black
Sharp ◄───────────	ACOUSTICS ───────────►	Dull

Chapter 5

Who will be involved in the MSE?

Introduction

Children with disabilities who require additional resources over and above those provided for mainstream children should become the focus of an individualised education plan (see Chapter 8). This plan is developed by a team, membership of which varies according to the needs of the child. The team usually consists of teaching and therapeutic professionals, and paraprofessionals as well as family members, including, whenever possible, the child.

The goal of the team is to ensure the child receives an appropriate education within the context of his or her disabilities. An appropiate education is one that fulfills four standards.

1. The child achieves at his or her highest potential.
2. The child is provided with an equal opportunity to learn in all curriculum areas, e.g. Braille for blind students, physical education for students with physical disabilities.
3. The focus of the curriculum is for the child to achieve self-sufficiency.
4. These programs must be accessible from the child's family home.

The MSE is one item on a menu of options that can be utilised by this team. The MSE option is distinct in character and has the potential to be a particularly valuable and rich addition to school life if it is used with care, intelligence and sensitivity. It is the responsibility of the team to make sure this potential is realised. This chapter identifies who are most likely to be involved in the MSE and then outlines a collaborative approach that these individuals could use when working together. The MSE team could be different to the IEP team because it could also include an expert in industrial design.

Organisation of the team

Several factors profoundly affect the efficiency of the team. The degree of availability of temporal, financial, material and human resources is fundamental. A suggested approach to best use of limited resources is a three-tiered system of team involvement, backed up by electronic technology for fast communication and permanent record-keeping. This three-tiered system of involvement is intended to maximise access to information without making undue time demands on the team, and to help keep costs to a minimum.

Level one involvement

This is of a general consultative nature, gathering information and opinions especially from those outside the team. The initial stages of identification, assessment, placement and determination of resource allocation could require the input of many allied professionals. Once such information had been gathered and initial decisions made, the number of people involved in ongoing management is usually substantially fewer.

In most countries it is a legal requirement that before testing can begin, informed parent or guardian consent is necessary. Often the legal requirement for testing stipulates the need for non-discriminatory evaluation. To be non-discriminatory, evaluation must be broadly based and sensitive to cultural factors. It needs to include test information validated for the specific purpose used, with more than one test taken from different disciplines when the results are used to inform placement and planning. Non-test information collected from family and significant others is also contributory.

Non-discriminatory evaluation is more likely to be achieved when assessment is overseen by a transdisciplinary, rather than a multidisciplinary, team. The term 'multidisciplinary' implies that professionals from a number of disciplines are involved but each professional works principally within his or her own discipline area. Collaboration therefore is at a secondary level and there is a danger that children with a disability can fall through the cracks between services. The term 'transdisciplinary' implies that the team uses collaboration at a primary level. This means that each team member works across discipline boundaries (Lacey and Lomas 1993; Orlove and Sobsey 1991).

Level two involvement

This is when the team develop the individualised education plan. The MSE programme would need to be written as an integrated part of the IEP (see Chapter 8). Ongoing management requires team members to meet regularly to revise and adapt the education plan in the light of feedback regarding the child's progress. The team is not static and over time people with different expertise will be involved at varying periods in the child's education.

Level three involvement

This involves the coordinator (often the special education teacher) overseeing the day-to-day, flexible, responsive implementation of the education plan.

The role of coordination may change depending upon the priorities identified by the transdiciplinary team. Occasional opportunities for MSE usage that fall outside the formally devised programme would need to be viewed on an individual basis.

Mutual respect and successful collaboration are essential for the optimal functioning of a special education team. Each member contributes particular knowledge, skills and attitudes that need to be recognised and appreciated by his/her colleagues. Those members of the team involved in MSE implementation are the MSE stakeholders.

Joint ownership and shared goals

As the challenges of special education have expanded, especially in relation to the increasing complexity of remit, so has desirability for a transdisciplinary interdependence within the special education team. The child's disabilities may be multiple and profound and the consequent needs diverse.

In line with a more holistic and ecologically sensitive approach, the special education teacher no longer has an authoritarian role and works in closely with a team that provides this transdisciplinary expertise. The process of the team working effectively together is often more difficult than initially assumed. Professions tend to have their own assumptions, their own discipline traditions and theoretical and philosophical approaches, as well as specialised skills. Individuals have their own idiosyncratic world views, so in order to be able to work in successfully together it is important that each team member has an understanding of the disciplines and viewpoints of the other team members. This is particularly important when working together in a common environment such as the MSE. Fulcher's (1989) ideas of discourse may be helpful to ensure that the team can respect each member's 'professionalism' while still working toward a common goal of 'democratisation' (p. 15).

The task for the team is to successfully address, in the widest sense, both the educational and health requirements of the child. This means that the medical model cannot be discarded entirely; a balance between the two needs to be determined. A common dilemma for the team is how to prevent the time demands of health care (specialist therapy interventions in particular) overwhelming the programme, at the expense of educational needs. Frequently, little time is left for organised, systematic instruction and for opportunities for learning through discovery. The MSE is a useful solution, as it is a way of providing therapy and specialised health care in a setting that can facilitate learning – to the mutual enrichment of both strands, if well handled. Furthermore the MSE can be used to provide educational opportunities in a setting that can facilitate therapy.

Traditionally, the classroom is a place where the teacher is in charge and where the focus is education. Traditionally, therapists have worked in a clinical setting, often in a separate room designed for that particular therapy. Recently these divisions have been challenged and therapists have begun to adopt a more integrated approach, both with one another and with the special education teacher. The MSE provides a unique opportunity for each professional to work together in a setting which is jointly owned. The MSE is not a classroom nor is it a clinic for therapy. Furthermore, it is a relatively new environment so it does not have the weight of tradition determining how it should be used. This means that all the stakeholders are free to collectively decide how best to use the space in a spirit of collaboration where they identify common goals and devise ways to cooperate that are consistent and effective.

Professional MSE stakeholders

Essentially there are five main types of professional involved in the MSE for a child with disability. They are the special education teacher, the physiotherapist, the occupational therapist, the communication therapist and the industrial design specialist. The teacher's aide is also likely to be a key member of the team. Depending upon the diverse needs of individual students there may be other individuals involved, usually at a consultative level (level one) rather than as an actual member of the team (level two). These could be other teachers (mainstream teachers or teachers with various specialisations), a psychologist or guidance officer, a social worker, medical practitioners of various specialisations, an optometrist, an orientation and mobility instructor, an audiometrist. This list is not exhaustive. The team needs to be small enough to maintain cohesion yet large enough to cover all required areas of expertise. Usually it is the role of the special education teacher to coordinate the team and to help ensure effective ongoing communication between team members.

The special education teacher

The special education teacher may work in a special school and be responsible for a class of children, all with special needs. Alternatively, the special education teacher may work in a mainstream school supporting children with special needs to attend mainstream classes. Other special education teachers may work part-time in a resource room and part-time in a regular school.

Despite these logistic and locational variations special education teachers have the same five major roles with regard to a student with a disability. They are: educator, student advocate, family–school liaison, member and co-ordinator of the special education team centred on that child, overseer of the programme decided on by this special education team (Gaylord-Ross and Holvoet 1985). In most cases the successful inclusion of the MSE in the child's education programme will be dependent upon the professional intelligence and sensitivity of the special education teacher in the role of coordinator of the child's education plan (level three). The special education teacher needs to have a wide range of special skills and insights regarding the child, the MSE and how other professionals' knowledge and skills can be integrated in optimal ways.

The physiotherapist

The ultimate goal of physiotherapy is to assist individuals 'to improve the quality of their life by achieving their optimum physical potential' (Moore, et al. 1994, p. 88). For a child with physical disability, the physiotherapist makes a full assessment of the child's chronic condition, together with any concomitant acute injury, in order to develop individualised action plans. Plans may consist of exercises for relaxation, stimulation, to strengthen muscle groups, improve balance, bear weight and to develop gross motor skills. The physiotherapist provides guidance and education for all team members, particularly family members, including, whenever possible, the child. The physiotherapist gives advice regarding good positioning (lying, sitting, standing, frequency of turning), good handling, range of motion, postural drainage, the use and construction of adaptive equipment, ergonomics and communication through movement.

Many physiotherapists see the MSE as beneficial to their work because a relaxing environment can make assessment and treatment more enjoyable for the child and therefore easier for the physiotherapist. The MSE can help the child gain sufficient confidence to try new activities and learn new skills under the physiotherapist's guidance. The MSE can facilitate the integration of the goals of physiotherapy with the goals of the other therapies and with those of education. The MSE

> . . . provides limitless opportunities for observation and subtle intervention. Clients who find it difficult to understand the purpose of activities/ required/desired during assessment, often do the activities naturally [in the MSE] . . . . The fact that activities are not stressful means that movements are not tense and artificial, giving a clearer picture of ability levels. (Moore et al. 1994, p. 94)

The physiotherapist needs to play a foundation role in the initial design and construction of the MSE in order to ensure that the environment is designed to maximise the opportunities for the child to improve his or her quality of life by achieving optimal physical potential.

The occupational therapist

The occupational therapist specialises in the development and maintenance of functions and skills necessary for daily living, especially fine motor functions and skills. Occupational therapists prescribe and administer treatments involved in developing adaptive skills for daily living tasks such as feeding, mouth movements, use of utensils and equipment, tolerance of textures, dressing, toileting and grooming. Attention is given to preventing degeneration of functions and helping to correct deficits that impair performance. The occupational therapist provides guidance and education for all team members, particularly the child's family including, whenever possible, the child, regarding the construction and use of fine motor adaptive equipment and conducting mealtime activities.

Occupational therapy has been at the forefront of MSE development. Many occupational therapists see the MSE as beneficial to their work because the environment can be used to both relax and stimulate the individual with a disability. The MSE helps to make assessment and treatment easier, more enjoyable and more successful. In parallel with physiotherapy, the MSE provides an ideal environment for occupational therapy guidance and education, for helping the child gain sufficient confidence to try new activities and learn new skills and for the integration of the goals of occupational therapy with the goals of the other therapies and education.

> All people need stimulation. In its absence, individuals may resort to self injury, anger or repetitive behaviour as a substitute. Therefore, the exposure to a wide range of sensory stimulation should be the cornerstone of treatment designed to reduce, avoid or channel these traits. Indeed, for those who have profound sensory, physical and mental disabilities, the only way of stimulating them and getting the brain to respond is through the primary senses. (Moore *et al.* 1994, p. 102)

The occupational therapist needs to play a foundation role in the initial design and construction of the MSE in order to ensure that the environment is designed to maximise opportunities for learning and development of functions and skills necessary for daily living.

The communication therapist

The communication therapist (usually called a speech-language pathologist or speech therapist) evaluates, diagnoses and treats speech and language disorders, assesses quality and quantity of sounds in the student's repertoire, and identifies other non-verbal means of communication. For children with severe communication disorders the role of the communication therapist is particularly important. Often the role of the communication therapist is closely linked in with physiotherapy, occupational therapy and special education.

Developing good communication skills is the principal aim of education. As many children with severe communication disorders rely on the use of movement for communication (i.e. through the use of sign or communication boards) learning how to communicate may directly involve the physiotherapists and occupational therapists. Furthermore because the anatomical and functional relationship between eating and speech overlap, some communication therapists develop expertise in assessing and facilitating mealtime skills (normally part of the occupational therapist's focus). The communication therapist plays a particularly important educational role with regards to teaching the child and the whole team, especially family members, the most appropriate methods of communication. When the child has a mild to moderate communication disorder the communication therapist is most likely to work in either a clinical or natural setting such as the regular classroom.

Many communication therapists see the MSE as beneficial to their work with children with severe communication disorders because it provides an excellent non-threatening environment for informal assessment and extended observation of interaction that is in context and rich in sensory experience. A particular strength of the MSE is that it enables communication therapy to become an extension of a leisure activity.

> A purpose built environment offers a secure, stimulating and exciting facility where learning new skills becomes fun. Although for some people verbal communication may not be an option, the use of multi-modal multi-sensorial stimulation can help effective functional communication to develop. Individuals may develop methods of effecting change expressing choice and feelings, of initiating and terminating a communication act or simply a way of saying, 'I'm here', 'I want to communicate with you'. (Moore *et al.* 1994, p. 102)

The communication therapist needs to play a foundation role in the initial design and construction of the MSE in order to ensure that the environment is designed to maximise opportunities for interacting with the environment and communicating with others.

The industrial design specialist

One only has to visit a MSE that has been designed by an expert in the field of industrial design to understand why it is beneficial to include this individual in the team from the beginning. The design specialist has possibly obtained qualifications in industrial psychology, architecture, visual arts and interior design. Industrial design is a sophisticated area in its own right. Some designers now further specialise in the disability field. Consequently such an individual would have access to the latest in design technology regarding play, leisure and recreation, therapeutic and learning environments for individuals with disabilities. The industrial design specialist helps to make dreams a reality and helps to ensure that the team is on the cutting edge of MSE design development.

Paraprofessional MSE stakeholders

The teacher's aide

Usually the teacher's aide works alongside and under the direction of the special education teacher. The teacher's aide often plays an active role in classroom daily functioning, including attending to children's physical health and comfort requirements, by handling and positioning individuals at set periods during the day and by helping in activities associated with education or therapy. The role of the teacher's aide in the MSE is extended to take on direction from the physiotherapist, the occupation therapist and the communication therapist.

Family MSE stakeholders

The most important person to be involved with the MSE is the child. The child's enthusiasm for the MSE is paramount. The MSE is only of value as an educational, therapeutic or recreational tool if there is an ongoing positive endorsement of MSE use. A vital feature of a successful MSE is that the child owns the place and the child owns the learning that goes on within its walls. This MSE is a place where the child has power and influence.

It is clearly beneficial if the MSE ethos is supported by the child's family or guardians *in loco parentis* (Berger 1991). Family involvement in the team must be voluntary with the levels of involvement self-determined by the individuals concerned. It is crucial that family members are made to feel they are equal and respected partners in the special education team (Gilbert and Low 1994). This will only occur if the family members genuinely feel that what they have to say is listened to, that what they have to offer is valued, and that they have power to influence and help shape what is being done at school with regard to their child. Factors that help to make the ideal a reality are:

- actively ensuring provision of adequate notice of meetings,
- seeking of informed consent with regard to decision making,
- ongoing encouragement to participate in the decision-making process,
- being fully informed of decisions made about their child, and
- being able to inspect and review their child's records and programme plans.

Family members (or guardians *in loco parentis*) have unique insights and expertise regarding their child and this knowledge must be recognised and incorporated into the overall programme. Involvement of the family from the planning stage through to the programme's inception and evaluation significantly increases the likelihood that the child will be receiving consistent and complementary intervention at home and school. Family members have the right to be coequal members of the team but, like all other members of the team, they also bear the responsibilities that such involvement entails.

Part of this responsibility entails being informed about the MSE. It may be necessary to provide the parents with explicit details regarding what is being done in the MSE and why. It cannot simply be assumed that parents will automatically develop positive attitudes towards the MSE and thereby be able to work in with the team. Some parents may have fairly limited views on the MSE and may need to be introduced to the more positive aspects of the MSE through an ongoing inservice education programme.

Regardless of the highest levels of expertise and caring, it is not possible for professionals within the team to adequately cater for all the child's social and emotional needs. Children with disabilities need to be viewed within an ecological perspective. They are sons or daughters, with parents or guardians and families who love them and care about their well-being. Furthermore they live in a community and need ample opportunities to interact with, and develop friendships with, other children. In addition to involvement of the family it is also desirable to include friends who are non-disabled in the child's MSE experience. The child is never simply a passive recipient of services. When thinking about who will be involved in the MSE it is best to keep the options wide and to be as inclusive as possible.

Collaboration

A child may need to work with a large number of professionals. In the past, these professionals tended to implement a service related to their discipline, without specifically considering wider ecological implications. This medical model approach was rejected by many service providers, and a more holistic approach that focuses globally on the needs of the child has been adopted. In this new approach, service providers work more closely with each other and with the family. Working together in a team, priorities can be identified and followed. Unnecessary overlap can be eliminated and interpersonal problem-solving can be employed to develop creative and integrated interventions (see Chapter 7). This transdisciplinary approach ensures that the child remains the centre of focus. Furthermore being in a team encourages '. . . a commitment from all members to keep up-to-date in their specialisms and maintain an "action research" attitude to their work' (Lacey and Lomas 1993, p. 5) so that their contribution can be at its most effective.

Friend and Cook (1992) defined interpersonal collaboration as 'a style for direct interaction between at least two coequal parties voluntarily engaged in shared decision making as they work toward a common goal' (p. 5). Their definition listed six characteristics as necessary for collaboration.

1. Involvement needs to be voluntary.
2. All participants need to be equal.

3. All participants share a common goal.
4. All are responsible for participation and decision-making.
5. All supply resources, and
6. All have accountability for outcomes.

For Friend and Cook, successful collaboration results in participants learning to value the style of interaction, developing trust in the other participants and feeling a sense of community with the other participants. This model of collaboration is directly applicable to the special education team. The intended result of such collaboration is a gestalt, where the whole is greater than the sum of its parts. Team members working closely together but in parallel are not able to provide those extra dimensions of density and richness that a collaborative approach can generate.

There are, however, barriers that make collaboration difficult to achieve. Lacey and Lomas (1993) identified: lack of 'training' in how to collaborate, administrative issues including separate funding, discipline traditions, shortages of resources – human, material, temporal, financial – frequently resulting in excessive workloads, status, codes of practice, confidentiality and individual preference to work autonomously. They further argued that collaboration could be made easier if there was increased support for collaboration both at legislative and managerial levels.

> When professionals act in good faith – toward one another and toward children and families – and make a commitment to better educational services for students with multiple disabilities, no barrier is permanent. Teams should not be fooled into believing that implementing the techniques and principles described . . . will be easy; the work is difficult. But the outcomes, both for children and professionals, justify the effort. (Orelove and Sobsey 1991, p. 28)

Collaboration in MSEs

Much of the current MSE literature talks about the need for staff to be 'trained' in how to use the MSE, raising the spectre of all the associations that 'training' implies, such as rigidity and formulaic staff-centred approach. Other papers talk of the original Dutch idea of staffing the MSE with the 'right kind of people', an infelicitous concept with wide-ranging repercussions. Overall, there is a most concerning dearth of literature regarding transdisciplinary collaboration in the MSE, indicating that transdisciplinary collaboration has not been widely adopted as a strategy for MSE use, although it is established in other areas of special education.

Yet transdisciplinary collaboration in the MSE has much to recommend it. It actively encourages the involvement of all staff in ongoing staff development within the context of the MSE. The sense of community engendered, where members value each other and respect the collaborative process as suggested by Friend and Cook, facilitates collaborative action research where critical analysis of theory and practice become a continuous process.

Winter (1996) described action research as providing 'the necessary link between self-evaluation and professional development' (p. 14). Action research as it relates to the MSE will be developed further in Chapter 11. Collaboration helps to ensure that team members become aware of their own biases and means that everyone's point of view is valued and deeply considered. Consequently, various accounts and critiques emerge to replace the single authoritative view of the past.

Chapter 6

Why focus on MSE design and construction?

Picture for a moment a time in your childhood when you were gloriously happy .... Where were you? What were you doing? Where were the adults? Whenever we ask people to do this they almost always report that they were in a free unstructured situation away from grown-ups. The more handicapped the child is, the less opportunity they have to experience the power of their independent movement. Helpfulness can sometimes prevent the child discovering for her[him]self. We learned this in infancy when we were unincumbered with adults. (Hopkins *et al.* 1994, p. 1)

Introduction

A fundamental aim of education is to enable the child to develop a concept of 'who am I?' (Parmenter 1992). An understanding of personal identity, the basis of ability to self-determine one's own future, is formed through ongoing active interaction with one's environment over an extended period of time. Most children seem to have an inbuilt thirst to find out who they are and to take control of their lives – to become increasingly more self-sufficient, autonomous. Their passage from childhood to adulthood is a natural unfolding process of discovery towards the gradual development of independence.

For some children with disabilities, however, this process of discovery must be engineered in ways that meet the child's particular needs, to prevent the process running out of momentum. If learning ceases, re-establishment requires highly specialised intervention, entailing making a neatness-of-fit match between the child's abilities and task difficulty. The specialist needs to have expert knowledge of how to engineer the child's environment to provide an appropriate background to these tasks.

The challenge is to engineer the environment in ways that enable the child to engage in the natural process of independent discovery learning. In the past, special educators often tried too hard, helped too much, which effectively denied the child the right to learn for him or herself. Transdisciplinary team members in the MSE see themselves as facilitators, with access to an environment that they can modify in ways that match the unique abilities of the child. Working closely together ensures that their observations of the child's abilities are as global and as accurate as can be possible.

Engineering the environment

Development of the concept of 'who am I' is a function of sensorimotor system activity (see Chapter 3). The sensorimotor system informs a complex, constantly changing map of oneself (body scheme) in relation to one's map of the environment. In order to more closely meet the particular ongoing needs imposed by a disability, the environment may need to be modified sympathetically. Pagliano (1997a) explains the rationale.

> The world of experience for non-disabled individuals is very different to that of the individual with severe multiple disabilities. For non-disabled individuals primary sensations (or the ability to experience taste, sight, smell, hearing, touch) are usually taken for granted because such sensations are integrated spontaneously and innately. However any assumption regarding the innate and spontaneous ability of individuals with severe multiple disabilities to integrate primary sensations must be deeply questioned. . . . Many individuals with severe multiple disabilities must learn to acquire the skill to experience primary sensations, in one or more sense areas. Furthermore these individuals may need vastly more opportunities than their non-disabled peers, to practice these skills to develop proficiency, to maintain skills over time, and to generalise them into everyday living. (pp. 89–90)

Environmental size and complexity are important (see Chapter 4). Some environments are too big or too complicated for some children with disabilities, with the result that these children become overwhelmed and confused, an impenetrable barrier to learning. Consequently for these children, smaller, less complicated environments are appropriate. For others (particularly older more experienced children), larger, more complicated environments may make a better match with their abilities. Educators need to be aware of environmental size and complexity and modify both according to the perceived needs of the child. These perceived needs can be identified through close observation of the way the child interacts with his or her environment, through maintaining precise records over time, through ongoing communication with all members of the team and through trial and error (educated guesswork). The less interaction the child makes with his or her environment the more likely it is that the child's environment is too large or too complicated or inappropriate in some other way.

Several types of rooms have been developed: the white room, the dark room, the soft play area, the interactive room, the sound room, the water room (see Chapter 4). These environments make it possible to isolate or combine stimuli, giving them variable prominence within a neutral ground. The sophisticated flexibility of such environments enables a considerable variety of task and task difficulty.

Many environmental dimensions can be modified. Several continua have already been described and included in summary sections at the end of Chapters 3 and 4. Further continua are to be found at the end of this chapter. These dimensions help to define the MSE in ways that may or may not be relevant to a particular child. By identifying as many relevant continua as possible, the transdisciplinary team members can engineer the MSE in more precise ways to match the child's interest and ability.

In Chapter 2, MSE-related literature was organised by type of environment. The 'single-minded' MSE describes a space that fulfils a single function whereas the 'open-minded' MSE describes a space that is multifunctional. The difficulty with the 'single-minded' space is that it only provides a neatness of fit for a particular type of child. On the other hand, the 'open-minded' space is actively designed to be modifiable to suit the particular needs of every child. In the single-minded space the child must fit the space whereas in the open-minded space the space fits the child. This notion of the space fitting the child sits comfortably with the educational definition of the MSE (see Chapter 1).

An environment to promote self-determination

Developing a concept of 'who am I?' is an essential precursor to developing personal fulfilment and autonomy. Mithaug (1991) identified six skill areas that promote the development of self-determination. Students become self-determined achievers when they:

1. become aware of their own needs, interests, and abilities;
2. learn self-direction by setting their own goals and developing their own plans;
3. gain self-confidence by increasing their skills and abilities to perform important tasks well;
4. become more self-reliant by learning to initiate 'risky actions' on their own;
5. increase their self-esteem by achieving intermediate successes in their talent areas;
6. take responsibility for positive and negative results by evaluating themselves objectively and then deciding what to adjust to improve next time. (p. xviii)

The MSE permits the child physical, emotional and intellectual space to develop at his or her own pace. Providing the catalyst to promote self-determination requires an imaginative repertoire of MSE teaching approaches. Development in Mithaug's six skill areas can be promoted in the MSE and will be further explored in the curriculum section (see Chapters 8, 9 and 10).

Learning styles

Learning style preference is a facet of the child's personality of which the transdisciplinary team members need to be aware, in order to tailor their approach best. The concept of learning style was developed in the 1960s by Dunn and Dunn (1992). While working in New York in regular schools, the Dunns began to investigate why different children would perform differently despite being taught using identical methods. This research led them to suggest that different people learn differently because they each have an individual learning style.

Dunn and Dunn (1992) described learning style as 'a biological set of personal characteristics that make the identical instruction effective for some students and ineffective for others' (p. 4). Their research indicated that 'when students are taught through their identified learning style preferences, they evidence statistically increased academic achievement, improved attitudes toward instruction, and better discipline than when they are taught through their nonpreferred styles' (p. 3).

The Dunns developed a learning style model which identifies a range of elements that may be used to define an individual's learning style. They are:

1. *immediate environment* (sound, light, temperature and furniture/seating designs);
2. *own emotionality* (motivation, persistence, responsibility [conformity versus nonconformity], and need for either externally imposed structure or the opportunity to do things in their own way);
3. *sociological preferences* (learning alone, in a pair, in a small group, as part of a team, or with either an authoritative or collegial adult; and wanting variety as opposed to patterns and routines);
4. *psychological characteristics* (perceptual strengths, time-of-day energy levels, and need for intake and/or mobility while learning); and
5. *processing inclinations* (global/analytic, right/left, and impulsive/reflective). (pp. 3–4)

The above model has been used to identify MSE continua, listed in Table 6.1 at the end of this chapter.

Some of the Dunns' ideas, especially those relating to processing inclinations continue to be challenged in the literature. There is a lack of evidence to support the use of generalisations. Many effective learning styles are influenced by the nature of the task being taught. Furthermore it would seem that those with more flexible learning styles have an increased facility to learn. Undoubtedly other factors, such as a child's health and physical comfort may influence a child's preferred learning style. Also learning style may change with age, experience and opportunity.

Despite these concerns Dunn and Dunn argue 'it is clear that people begin to concentrate, process, and remember new and difficult information under very different conditions' (pp. 5–6). Exactly how or why these differences occur is not fully understood. What is known is that learning for an individual is enhanced by an appropriate environment and mode of presentation of material or task type.

Getting an accurate idea of the learning style strengths and preferences of a child with a disability is often not easy. Careful sensitive observation is essential. Dunn and Dunn (1992) make six assumptions that could be used by the transdisciplinary team when working in the MSE. They are:

1. individuals can learn;
2. individuals have different strengths (preferences) in learning;
3. preferences can be measured/identified;
4. students attain higher achievement and attitudes in matched rather than mismatched situations;
5. teachers can learn to use learning styles as a cornerstone to their instruction;
6. students can learn to capitalise on own learning style strengths. (p. 6)

The aim is to design a more effective and efficient learning environment for each individual child. The physical environment is obviously crucial, but so too are the child's emotionality, sociological preferences and psychological characteristics (Lewis and Doorlag 1987).

To design learning environments for children with severe communication difficulties particularly those unable to make decisions for themselves, educators must work together using the most sophisticated educational technology and assessment methods available (Light 1989; Crossley 1992; Light and McNaughton 1993; Mirenda and Calculator 1993). These include the use of micro indicators such as absence of crying or distress and conducting surveys to identify the likes and dislikes of children of similar age, gender and circumstance.

Quality of life

Quality of life (QOL) was described by Shalock (1988) as the 'human service issue of the next few decades'.

QOL has emerged as an important outcome measure in the disability field. This is because of the dissatisfaction both with the previous almost exclusive use of objective quantitative measures and also with the over emphasis on education as preparation for employment, often to the exclusion of education for other more practical areas such as leisure and life skills (Cummins 1992).

QOL, being subjective, eludes a precise universal definition. Quality for one person may not be valued as such by someone else (Taylor and Bogdan 1990; Goode 1990). Individuals may experience similar circumstances very differently. Nevertheless a QOL focus provides an ideal that helps to delineate desired outcomes and enables the transdisciplinary team to create a shared vision for the individual who is using the MSE (Halpern 1989).

Halpern (1994) listed the following QOL domains:

- physical and material wellbeing,
- performance of a variety of age-appropriate roles, and
- a sense of personal fulfilment.

Halpern listed areas for particular attention as:

- promoting self-determination,
- developing a full array of instrumental programmes,
- enhancing inclusive instructional environments, and
- improving the range of available community resources.

The MSE can play an important role in promoting QOL for individuals with profound, multiple disabilities by expanding his or her range of experiences and interactions. The MSE has a role in each of Halpern's three domains and in promoting self-determination. The first three Halpern areas for particular attention are the concern of the IEP team, of which the MSE is a part (see Part III). The last is an equity issue depending on the will of the wider community.

Age-appropriate

As well as being level-appropriate, it is important that MSE design and construction is age-appropriate.

To be age-appropriate the MSE must include in its design and construction aspects which are reasonable for the person's chronological age. An unfortunate handicapism has been to treat people with disabilities as 'forever children'. This has meant that some people with disabilities have been treated as if they were children long after they have reached adulthood. Wolfensberger (1984) cautioned that it was especially important to ensure that individuals vulnerable to being devalued were not presented in ways that made them look and appear younger than their chronological age.

The MSE must include in its design and construction aspects which are generally valued by children of a similar age. However it is not uncommon for adults who work in segregated situations over extended periods of time to have no direct ongoing contact with children of similar age in the mainstream.

Therefore active efforts need to be made to seek out information about what age peers really like and ensure that the MSE includes items which are part of the peer group's cultural capital.

Value-appropriate

To be value-appropriate, the MSE must incorporate in its design, construction and use aspects which are reasonable for the society in which we live. The MSE is used as an integral part of a curriculum, founded on a framework of equity and social justice values (see below). Awareness and acceptance of these values by the transdisciplinary team is mandatory if the criticism is to be avoided of the MSE 'being used for containment, or as a dumping ground where people with learning difficulties are placed and ignored' (Mount and Cavet 1995, p. 54).

Equity and social justice

Equity is fundamental to social justice. The concept of social justice is attributed to Rawls (1971), who argued that because justice requires impartiality, discrimination against any disadvantaged subgroup is unacceptable. This concept of social justice has widespread ramifications, reaching into all areas of social activity. In some countries social justice principles have been enshrined in law, for example PL 94–142 in the USA. In reality though, fully-fledged social justice is unattainable. Starr (1991) cautioned that social justice is 'always controversial in theory and imperfect in practice. . . . Some kinds of social justice are just not achievable because they are at odds with the political and economic forces which shape our society' (p. 24).

Dyson (1997, p. 155) also argued that 'many problems which manifest themselves in the education system . . . are connected to patterns of disadvantage and inequity in society as a whole'. He called these 'difficulties *in* education but not, primarily *of* education'. He claimed that 'although education may be inadequate in addressing these difficulties, it may have a role to play, as part of a much broader social and economic strategy, in creating a more equitable society'.

This does not mean that the ideals of social justice are not worth pursuing vigorously, especially with regard to the problem of inequity in education (Hatton and Elliot 1994). A basic social justice principle in education was summed up by Connell (1990). You take 'the standpoint of the least advantaged . . . . You think out the educational strategies that are in their interests; and implement them' (p. 9). The goal is to achieve equity of the advantaged and disadvantaged. At a profound level the MSE can contribute to equity for children with disabilities by promoting quality of life, a human right, a universal goal for all children.

Conclusion

The rationale for specific and global approaches to MSE design and construction has been discussed. It is important to view the MSE in not only educational and therapeutic contexts but also in its wider social context. It is less likely that children will experience developmental delays beyond those directly associated with their disabilities if educators of children with severe multiple disabilities 'understand the consequences of multisensory demands and . . . structure environmental sensory stimulation to promote optimal, meaningful use of the residual . . . [sense] capacity' (Morse 1990, p. 202).

> Individuals with severe multiple disabilities experience delays in cognitive development, motor development, and social skills beyond those directly associated with their disabilities, because of lack of motivation or insufficient opportunities to explore their environments actively (O'Donnell and Livingston 1991). The MSE was found to be highly motivational and to offer abundant opportunities to experience primary sensations. Documentation of successful student outcomes should extend beyond quantitative performance measures to include qualitative indicators. One such example of life quality measure is defined as the extent of effective behaviours an individual has (Evans and Scotti 1989). The rationale of use of the MSE with individuals with severe multiple disabilities is based on recognition that the perception of sounds, lights, shadows, scents and touch are vitally important experiences in their own right. Increased ability to integrate primary sensation greatly enhances quality of life for individuals with severe multiple disabilities (Ulrich 1991). (Pagliano 1997a, p. 90)

Table 6.1 Continua identified in Chapter 6

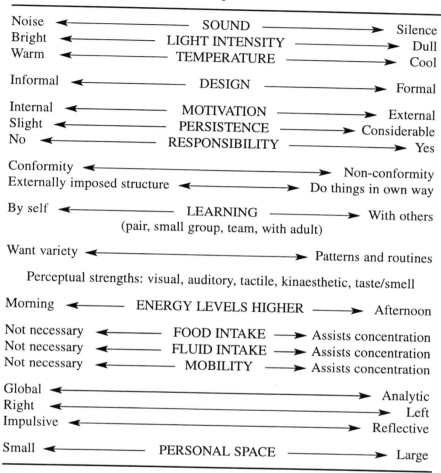

Chapter 7

How to design and construct a MSE

Introduction

The planning of the design and construction of a MSE requires much preparation and attention to detail. There is a limited amount of well-conducted research available to support decisions. A stage by stage approach is recommended to ensure a solid foundation, to result in a MSE appropriate for its users over several years.

Planning

Stage one

This involves making certain that all the potential stakeholders, members of the future transdisciplinary team, genuinely understand what a MSE is. In practice, this process is led by school staff members, who identify the interested individuals. Information is obtained via literature searches, visiting MSEs in action and spending time in the MSE, talking to staff and students who currently use the MSE. Understanding needs to be sophisticated, not merely in terms of what equipment can be used. There needs to be a sense of the strengths and limitations of the MSE, an awareness of the specific and global rationales for various approaches to using the MSE. Information is made available to all by starting a staff library on the topic (books, journal articles, videos), by running seminars and encouraging discussion.

Stage two

This involves ensuring that school staff have a clear idea of who the students are that might use the MSE, and why. There are several questions to be answered. What do the staff currently know about these students, through what level of assessment? How is it anticipated that student needs will be met by the MSE? What is the current whole-school curriculum, policy and philosophy and how will the MSE fit in? Is the school population changing over time? If so, in what way and how will these changes impact on MSE use?

All these considerations are used to inform the planning of MSE design and construction. Stages one and two are ongoing processes throughout MSE use.

Stage three

This involves identifying what funds could be available to build and maintain the MSE, either within the current budget or through special funding. Some companies offer 'advice, design, planning, installation' (ROMPA 1997, p. 8). Others offer a 'free fund raising package' consisting of a business plan 'which covers the concepts, costs and information that local businesses . . . [funding bodies may] be interested to know', as well as a promotion video, information leaflet, fund raising thermometer and posters (TFH 1997, p. 3). The significant disadvantage in using commercial services is that the MSE is tied to the commercial vision, not that of the transdisciplinary team. A possible alternative is to include a freelance industrial design specialist in the transdisciplinary team. This individual could be responsible for coordinating the design and construction of the MSE while ensuring that it matches the requirements of each team member (see Chapter 5).

Stage four

This involves (usually the staff) making the decision to either go ahead and build a MSE, to put the project on hold or to reject it altogether. Ayres (1994) advised prospective MSE designers to deeply question personal motives for wanting to build a MSE in the first place. 'It is very important that it is right for your clients and represents good value for money' (Ayres 1994, p. 29). If the decision is in the affirmative, a working group needs to be convened. This working group should comprise as many representatives of the projected transdisciplinary team as possible.

A seven-step interpersonal problem-solving algorithm could be used. Steps are:

1. preparation
2. problem identification
3. generation of potential solutions
4. evaluation of potential solutions
5. implementation of solutions, and
6. evaluation of outcome.

As a precursor, it is necessary for each team member to actively be aware of his or her own personal values, philosophies, preferences and frame of reference. This self-awareness enables each team member to recognise and respect the individual differences of each other member. In order to respect this diversity of opinion, interpersonal relationships within the team need to be considered separately from the tasks of problem-solving. For if these two concepts are not isolated from each other constructive comments could be misconstrued as personal criticism and individuals may find it difficult to work together.

During problem identification, the problem must be separated from the solution. If an individual describes a problem and includes a solution at the same time others will feel excluded from the problem-solving process. Other barriers which jeopardise group interaction are individuals:

- categorising suggestions made by others,
- making judgements about suggestions,
- changing the suggestions of others before they have been discussed,
- experimenting with the ideas of others before the group have had time to process those ideas, and
- manipulating the meeting by introducing surprise information that was not previously available to the rest of the team.

Techniques to help generate potential solutions include:

- brainstorming (oral),
- brainwriting (written),
- lateral thinking,
- idea checklist,
- each team member taking it in turns to lead the discussion,
- each team member taking on specific but separate task.

Once potential solutions have been identified each needs to be evaluated. This involves delineating the positives, neutrals and negatives for each possible solution. This evaluation then leads on to the job of selecting the most reasonable solution, establishing responsibilities and preparing a timeline. Implementing the solution comprises finalising plans, describing criteria for success, detailing evaluation and the actual implementation. The final step involves the evaluation which then leads on to a new cycle or closure.

Stage five

This involves making a detailed cost estimate. MSEs can range in price from very expensive to quite cheap – depending on the size and complexity of the room and on who builds it, a commercial company or friends of the school. When inviting commercial companies to tender, Ayres (1994) warns 'Do not mistake salesmanship for good advice – the two are not always compatible' (p. 30). As well as building and stocking, the cost estimate should also include hidden expenses such as ongoing maintenance and repair. The MSE is likely to be expensive in other ways too, especially in staff time – up to hundreds of hours if each member of the transdisciplinary team is fully involved in the design process. However, time spent in planning is repaid when the MSE functions as envisaged without hitches.

Stage six

This involves finalising the funding in the light of the cost estimate and deciding whether the MSE will be built all at once or in stages. Clearly if the MSE is to be built all at once, the funding will be required up front, whereas if the MSE is to be built in stages the funding could be spread out over a much longer time period. Regardless of the timeframe of the construction, it is necessary to plan the final environment from the beginning so that, when complete, it fulfils all the desired functions, avoiding costly alterations being made down the track.

Health and safety

Another important area of planning involves considering health and safety issues. There are no formal guidelines for MSEs specifically, but the MSE must comply with the local health and safety regulations for schools generally. It is advisable to keep formal documentation with regard to this compliance. Documentation should also be made of all events within the MSE, for example keeping a record sheet of MSE bookings and usage. All breakages, leaks, spills, accidents and malfunctions should be reported immediately for attention.

In the planning stages, once the room has been chosen and a draft design has been developed, the transdisciplinary team will need to seek formal advice to check that the MSE design has no hidden dangers. It is also advisable to maintain a programme of regular safety checks when the MSE is up and running to make sure that new unpredicted dangers are not developing.

Ask a structural engineer to check the room to ensure that it is indeed structurally sound for its intended purpose. This involves identifying what heavy and weight-bearing equipment is projected for the MSE and examining where such equipment will be located to see if the floor, ceiling or walls require additional reinforcing. It may be planned, for instance, to have chairs that hang from the ceiling, or pulleys and levers to move people in wheelchairs from one location to another. The structural engineer advises how best to do this. In practice, it is cheaper to modify the MSE design to fit in with the room, rather than the other way around. For example it might be suggested that the water bed is moved into the corner so that it could rest on two major support beams rather than be located near the door where it would rest on just one beam.

Ask an electrical engineer to be involved in the planning early on. The MSE may require many electrical power points – 24, six on each wall is not unusual – and the electricity supply must be adequate to cope with demand. A master switch is a helpful addition, so the last person to leave the room can easily and confidently switch everything off, without having to check every individual piece of equipment. Pay particular attention to the location of power points. They need to be easily accessible but in positions safe from probing hands and tools. Circuit breakers are useful and cheap; they cut the current supply if the equipment is faulty. It is best not to have equipment and lighting on the same circuit, for otherwise if one piece of equipment failed, tripping the circuit breaker, the whole room would be plunged into darkness. Consideration needs to be given to the need for the provision of emergency electricity in the event of a power cut. All electrical equipment must be safety checked at least once a year, and ideally earthed and/or double insulated to minimise risk of electrocution. Obviously all pieces of equipment should be kept on stable surfaces where they cannot be knocked over or pulled off.

A third consideration is ventilation. The usual MSE is cut off from the outside world, without windows, so it needs its own ventilation. The ideal is a high-quality air conditioning system that is quiet, with both heating and cooling facilities. Between sessions the room should be opened up for comprehensive airing to help rid the MSE of stale smells.

A fourth consideration is cleaning the MSE and keeping it hygienic. Usually there are local authority guidelines that are relevant to developing a basic cleaning programme. The manufacturers give advice on how to clean their equipment. Ideally the MSE needs to have a dedicated cleaning team, who clean the room on a regular basis and who have an understanding of the special nature of the MSE room. It would be sensible to consult with the cleaning staff during the design and construction stage to get their input early re cleaning practicalities and pitfalls. Preference needs to be given to fittings that are waterproof and that can be easily removed for washing or, failing that, are disposable. Inevitably there will be accidents on occasion, such as vomiting, defaecation, micturition, and these need to be thought through. How can the ball pool, soft play area, water bed or other equipment be easily and effectively cleaned in these situations? The local hospital microbiology department may be a useful advice resource. Whenever possible the cleaner should avoid the use of strong chemicals for several reasons – they can be toxic, some people may experience allergies, while for others it may interfere with MSE activities such as aromatherapy. If such chemicals are used, the equipment needs to be well rinsed. Not using strong chemicals needs to be balanced against the risk of disease transmission in a vulnerable population. Any water that is in contact with MSE users, such as in water rooms, needs major decontamination, such as via chlorination. Water in equipment not in contact with MSE users, such as in bubble tubes, needs to be disinfected and/or changed regularly.

A fifth consideration is fire safety. The local fire service need to be consulted during the planning stages. The MSE should be fitted with a smoke detector and house at least one fire extinguisher. Room furnishings, equipment and materials lining the room walls, ceiling and floor should comply with fire safety regulations, including being made of fire-retardant non-toxic materials. It is a good idea to have more than one exit, especially if the room is going to be occupied by several people at once, some with poor mobility. All exits need to be clearly marked and able to be opened easily at all times. There should be a fire safety evacuation plan clearly visible, known and regularly rehearsed by all staff using the MSE. This fire safety evacuation plan could be part of a general emergency action plan to be put into operation if any serious problem occurs.

A sixth consideration is ease of access and movement within the room. The room needs to be designed with the special requirements of various individuals with various disabilities in mind. For wheelchair users there need to be clear doorways of wheelchair width in and out of the room. There need to be wide pathways within the room leading to each piece of equipment. Equipment needs to be of appropriate height. It is also important to think about the personal safety of staff especially when involved in lifting. Particular countries have set regulations that need to be followed. If children with visual impairments are going to use the room, it would be a good idea to consult early in the planning process with an orientation and mobility specialist. Modifications might include the use of tube lighting on pathways and the use of different textures on the floor signifying different areas. It is important to be aware that movement of equipment within the MSE can be confusing to children with disabilities. Finding the right balance on the constancy and change continuum requires astute observation of the needs of individual children.

A seventh consideration is the goal of being able to ensure the personal safety and comfort of each individual child. No deterioration should result from being in the MSE. For example, no dangerous pulsing light should be used in the MSE because it may trigger epilepsy in susceptible individuals. The MSE may not be suitable for children who are claustrophobic. No child should be in the room by him or herself. It would be advisable to have an emergency phone extension in the MSE room. All staff should be taught cardio-pulmonary resuscitation.

The safe, intelligent, responsible use of the MSE depends on the transdisciplinary team collaborating and taking advice when appropriate. Carefully assessing the children with regards to safety of access to the multisensory activities is essential. Keeping impeccable ongoing records helps the process and facilitates review.

Lighting

An eighth consideration is that of lighting. Lighting effects are very important for creating an atmosphere within the MSE and can also be extremely practical, like for making movement into, within and out of the room easier, especially for those with visual impairment. Lighting *per se* is required for cleaning and maintenance.

There is a wide range of lighting that can be used in the MSE. These include regular lighting (with dimmer), UV lighting, projected lighting, spot-lighting with mirror or sparkle ball, special effects lighting (plasma lamp, sound-light wall or floor) and fibre-optic lighting. As a general rule, lighting should be positioned well away from fabrics and all other potentially flammable items, particularly plastic surfaces.

Lighting also needs to be positioned well away from the children using the MSE, to avoid dazzle, burns and electrical accidents. A possible exception to this rule is the fibre-optic spray. Although the fibre-optic light source still needs to be positioned well away, the fibre-optic tail can be touched and played with by the child, within limits. Cavet and Mount (1995) warn that

> Anyone using the fibre optic 'tail' should never be allowed to put the ends of the strands into their mouths, as these are made from glass fibre. These fibres are perfectly safe to handle in an ordinary way, and may even be draped around someone or bent quite sharply to change the pattern of light, but like any other electrical equipment they must be treated with respect. (p. 77)

The issues surrounding the use of UV lighting have received considerable coverage in the MSE literature, despite there being a minimal risk to safety. Diffey (1993) stated that provided UV black light lamps are 'used properly' they are 'safe and pose no risk to health' (p. 10). UV radiation forms an invisible part of the electromagnetic spectrum and has a wavelength of 200–400 nanometres. (A nanometre (nm) is one thousand millionth of a metre.)

There are three bands of UV radiation: UVA (320–400 nm), UVB (290–320 nm), and UVC (200–290 nm). Fortunately the lamps used in the MSE do not produce UVB, largely responsible for sunburn and skin cancer, nor UVC, very dangerous to the eyes and skin, in significant amounts. However the four-foot blacklight lamps used in the MSE do produce UVA radiation. These lamps look purple when switched off and are lilac surrounded by a fuzzy haze when switched on.

UVA radiation is found naturally in sunlight. It is about 20 times more intense than UVB but much less harmful. Very high doses over a long period of time are needed to cause skin or eye damage. The intensity of the UVA radiation quickly weakens as distance from the lamp increases (see Table 7.1). Precautions when using blacklight lamps include positioning the lamp as far as possible from the user, limiting use in small MSEs, checking lamps using a nanometer to ensure they are within the 315–400 nm range, installing a timer on the lamp, avoiding lamp reflection, inhibiting direct eye gaze at lamps and encouraging children to remain fully clothed when using UV lighting.

Table 7.1 Distance from UV light source, time exposed, given in equivalent times in sunlight (Diffey 1993, p.11)

Distance from blacklight lamps	Time exposed to UV lamps				
	10 mins	30 mins	1 hour	2 hours	4 hours
6 inches	50 secs	2.5 mins	5 mins	10 mins	20 mins
1 foot	25 secs	75 secs	2.5 mins	5 mins	10 mins
2 feet	10 secs	30 secs	1 min	2 mins	4 mins
4 feet	4 secs	12 secs	24 secs	48 secs	96 secs
8 feet	1 sec	3 secs	6 secs	12 secs	24 secs

Aesthetics

Once the practical considerations have been attended to, the next task is to pay particular attention to the aesthetics of the room. Kewin (1994a) argued that the MSE 'must be inviting and comfortable whilst providing stimulation in an adaptable and acceptable way. Choice and control over aspects of the environment should be included where appropriate' (p. 10). He made a number of helpful recommendations regarding setting up a white room. They are:

1. access – leave the entrance clear. In large rooms consider a track;
2. comfort/safety – cushioning – essential on the floor – less essential on walls. Wedges add quality and comfort;
3. lighting: (a) projector with effect wheels (b) spot lamps – static – colours (c) disco spot lamp – changing colours (d) mirror ball (rotates) – goes with disco spot lamp;
4. focal point – a bubble tube or fibre optic spray;
5. sounds – speakers or safely placed tape player (constant play facility);
6. walls – white or magnolia to reflect pastel shades;
7. mobiles – add interest and change light effects. (p. 17)

There is a tendency for non-disabled people to primarily consider aspects of visual beauty when considering aesthetics. But a multisensory environment must have a multisensory aesthetic. It needs to appeal to all the senses, both each sense on its own and in combination. To help MSE design, it might be helpful to blindfold each member of the transdisciplinary team so he or she can identify how the room sounds, smells, tastes, feels, so he or she can get an idea of the sense of space, the non-visual logic of the room, the energy, the ambience.

Another approach would be to invite a blind person to check out the MSE and listen carefully to his or her observations. What does that individual like and dislike about the room? What suggestions does the person have to improve the room? Likewise invite others with disabilities and find out how they respond.

Use of themes

The use of themes (underwater, space) can help to liven up a MSE that is starting to lose its appeal. Themes can encourage a much more creative use of the environment and can help to integrate MSE activities with the curriculum. Hirstwood and Gray (1995) suggested for example that 'Religious festivals can ... be portrayed and experienced more sensitively using a theme approach' (p. 32). One teacher talked of having a Christmas tree with lights attached to a switch for the child to control. Pagliano (1997a) described an adventure teaching episode where the children were involved in an alien space invasion. Some of the children became so engrossed in the game that they engaged in interaction in ways not previously observed by the teachers or therapists (see Chapter 10).

Getting the MSE built and beyond

Ayres (1994) reminded prospective MSE designers that the work does not simply cease once the plan has been finalised. There is still much to be done during the construction phase.

> When you've gone through the processes and are physically constructing your environment, continual discussion and monitoring are necessary to ensure you get what you want, where you want it and to the standard you want. Don't be afraid to be critical, it's your valuable funds after all. ... It is most important that everyone who has access understands and can operate the equipment constructively and safely. (p. 30)

Hirstwood and Gray (1995) recommended that an inventory be made of all equipment to be housed in the MSE. This inventory 'should cover a description of each item, how to use it, how to maintain it, how to repair it, or what to do if it can't be repaired and needs to go back to the manufacturer or suppliers' (p. 48). The inventory is cumulative, growing as people suggest new uses for particular pieces of equipment.

Table 7.2 Continua identified in Chapter 7

Constancy ←————————————————————→ Change

PART III:
Curriculum development

Chapter 8

Curriculum development and the MSE

The curriculum is an ever changing entity. It must reflect the current climate in schools and the wider community. In order that it may fulfil its main purpose, that of providing a sound education as a right of all pupils, it is essential that staff within these schools learn from one another and share their experiences and ideas. (Byers and Rose 1996, p. 12)

Introduction

The lack of a substantial MSE research literature base means there is little current information available to support the development of curriculum specifically related to the MSE. Therefore it is necessary to build a curriculum for the MSE from the ground up. This entails establishing an overall curriculum infrastructure and then fitting a range of MSE approaches into the ethos. It is not possible at present to frame any specific MSE approach within any particular educational system (such as the National Curriculum). This development is yet to come.

Curriculum development for the MSE will specifically be for children with learning difficulties. A child is said to have a learning difficulty if, because of a disability, impairment or disorder, he or she is unable to receive an appropriate education (see Chapter 5) without additional and/or different educational services than those provided for the majority of children of the same age. Special education provision describes those services that are additional or different.

Children who have special learning needs because of factors other than disability, such as poverty, isolation or ethnic background are not included in the learning difficulty definition. Educational services for these children may however, follow a similar logic to that used in special education (see 'The curriculum and social justice' below). Furthermore, once the benefits of the MSE are substantiated, curriculum development for the MSE may expand into the mainstream curriculum and be used in the wider school population (see Chapter 12).

The regular curriculum

The term 'curriculum' generally describes the course of study being conducted by a student at school. In its broadest sense the curriculum

> ... has to do with teaching and learning activities across many domains (knowledge, skills, values and attitudes), and especially with the scope and nature of student experiences as set out by society generally and specifically by educational authorities, principals, and teachers. The dominant form of curriculum is that which is devised by educational authorities with reference to the age of students (or the number of years they have attended school), often with regard to the diversity of student achievements at any particular age or grade level. In some cases the curriculum is formulated as little more than a syllabus (or list of topics to be taught), while in others the curriculum takes the form of broad guidelines, which are meant to be interpreted by teachers in the light of local circumstances and the characteristics of particular students. (Elkins 1997, p. 86)

Different countries approach curriculum differently, but all educational systems can identify a 'dominant form of curriculum', stipulating what will be taught to the majority of children of compulsory school age. What form this should take is often debated. Furthermore, there is a corollary that in addition to the stated curriculum, there is a 'hidden' curriculum of issues that are not raised. Omissions and silences give a message: that certain ways of knowing are recognised and valued while others are not.

It is intrinsic to the regular curriculum that it cannot alone deliver equity, as it is designed to cater for the majority of students, not for all. To cater for the needs of all students, particularly those who are disadvantaged, the regular curriculum requires input from other sources. These sources include the use of curricular options from social justice and/or from special education. They are: compensatory, oppositional, counter-hegemonic, supportive, modified and alternative curricula. Generally speaking, the MSE curriculum will be outside that of the regular curriculum but will have direct application within the six listed curricular options.

The curriculum and social justice

In education the use of the term 'social justice' is attributed to the work of Rawls (1971) who argued that justice is built on impartiality. Rawls maintained that in education discrimination against any subgroup of the population, including those with disabilities, is unacceptable because such an educational service is not impartial. More recently many countries have introduced legislation to protect the rights of individuals susceptible to being disadvantaged. Separate legislation to protect the rights of individuals with disabilities often exists.

Connell (1990) identified the fundamental principle of social justice in education as taking 'the standpoint of the least advantaged . . . . You think out the educational strategies that are in their interests; and implement them' (Connell 1990, p. 9). Connell described three curriculum logics that could be used to redress disadvantage in education.

1. The compensatory curriculum where extra resources are provided to schools serving students who are disadvantaged. The goal of the compensatory curriculum is to enable the student to gain improved access to the regular curriculum. For example, students with visual impairment may require extra resources, both human and material, in order to learn Braille, orientation and mobility and more sophisticated skills of listening. A dark MSE compensatory curriculum topic could be to teach the student with low vision to best use remaining vision (see Chapter 9).

2. The oppositional curriculum is based on the rejection of the logic of the regular curriculum. The goal of the oppositional curriculum is to devise a curriculum that 'really suits' those students who have been disadvantaged by the regular curriculum. An example of this would be a segregated special school curriculum for Deaf students built entirely on the use of British Sign Language (BSL) taught within a context of Deaf culture. There are clearly oppositional curriculum uses of the MSE, particularly when teaching children with severe/profound multiple learning difficulties (see Chapter 10).

3. The counter-hegemonic curriculum is the most radical. The goal of the counter-hegemonic curriculum is to reconstruct the regular curriculum so that disadvantage is no longer seen as outside the mainstream and separate but rather as part of the regular spectrum. A more inclusive curriculum is thereby generated. This is achieved by inviting members from relevant subgroups to help develop the curriculum. For example if the school has students with physical disabilities, adults with physical disabilities would be invited to be a part of the curriculum development from its inception. Inviting adults with disabilities to help design the MSE curriculum could be a very fruitful process. The MSE could well become part of the mainstream curriculum if a counter-hegemonic curriculum were to be adopted.

Giorcelli (1993) used counter-hegemonic curriculum logic to define a good school. A good school is

a school that is successful in teaching all of its students the essential learnings and skills they need to know or to be able to apply. If the focus of the school is on *quality* and *equity*, the outcome indicators selected to demonstrate student achievement should reflect with accuracy the curriculum being taught, and the outcome results should be examined in such a way that educators can be certain that no major subset of the student population is left behind. (p. 85)

Curriculum logics can be used separately or in combination. They can also be used to teach the same material – the difference being in the rationale used to support and develop the curriculum. The use of a number of different curricula may provide a disadvantaged student with increased opportunities.

For example, a blind student may attend his or her local community school and study a regular curriculum. As Braille is not taught as part of the regular curriculum, a compensatory curriculum may be necessary to ensure that the student maintains high level Braille skills. The focus of such tuition would be to ensure that the student has full access to the regular curriculum. Tuition could occur outside normal school hours or during school hours if the student drops a non-essential part of the regular curriculum. An oppositional curriculum in Braille may be offered at summer school attended by a group of Braille using blind students. The focus of the oppositional curriculum might be to study Braille within a blind cultural context.

Alternatively, the regular school curriculum may be reconstructed by a school council to include Braille as part of the regular curriculum. This may involve the school providing lessons in both print and Braille by a teacher proficient in both. Such a student may still benefit from the insertion of a summer school oppositional curriculum where Braille is studied with other blind students.

The curriculum and special education

Ashman and Elkins (1997) described special education as having four features. Special education

> . . . is a relative concept, defined in terms of what *additional* programs and resources are needed to provide an appropriate education for students. If a school provides programs and resources needed by certain children with disabilities as a matter of course, this would not be regarded as special education. . . .
> . . . requires a flexible and innovative approach to teaching which focuses on the individual . . .
> . . . is a testing ground for innovative teaching strategies and techniques . . .
> . . . has a unique economic and political character. (p. 7–8)

The attraction of the regular curriculum is that it is developed for the vast majority of students and therefore is age-appropriate. The attraction of a special education curriculum is that it is specifically developed for an individual student and therefore is level-appropriate and medium-appropriate. The goal for a student with special needs is for both curricula to work together within a social justice context, to provide the best available individualised option at each point in time. This option however needs to be constantly assessed and reassessed by all major stakeholders in the special education team.

Special education curriculum options relate to the placement and the specific needs of a particular student (see Table 8.1). Seven possible placement options for students with learning difficulties are:

1. full regular school inclusion without support;
2. regular school inclusion with special education teacher support;
3. regular school inclusion with part-time resource room access;
4. resource room access with part-time regular school inclusion;
5. self-contained full-time resource room access in regular school;
6. segregated day school;
7. residential school.

These placement options give rise to six curriculum options: regular, compensatory, oppositional, counter-hegemonic (as described above); supported; modified; alternative.

The supported curriculum is used when the student studies more than 50per cent but less than 100 per cent of the regular curriculum. The gap is then filled with a special-education-designed-curriculum aimed at helping the student better manage those parts of the regular curriculum that are being studied. The goal of the supported curriculum is to repackage priority parts of the regular curriculum so that it more closely matches the learning style needs of the student with learning difficulties. Placement therefore is primarily in the regular classroom with part-time learning support. The supported curriculum does not include additional material to that being studied in the regular curriculum. A student may study regular, supported and compensatory curricula. For example, a Braille using student may find the regular curriculum alone too difficult and may need a supported curriculum in key learning areas.

The modified curriculum is used when the student studies less than 50 per cent but more than 25 per cent of the regular curriculum. The majority of the regular curriculum therefore has been simplified to make the work level appropriate. Topics are taken from the regular curriculum in order to keep the tasks age-appropriate. Placement therefore is primarily in a special education facility but some time is spent in the regular classroom. The modified curriculum is more likely to be used if the student has more than one disability.

The alternative curriculum is used when the student studies more than 75 per cent of the special education curriculum. Here the focus of the curriculum is development of life skills. Placement is usually in a segregated special education facility. The alternative curriculum is more likely to be used if the student has severe to profound multiple disabilities and might only be able to learn a very limited number of new skills. The alternative curriculum is different to the oppositional curriculum because the goal of the oppositional curriculum is to be as broad and as deep as the regular curriculum.

In Table 8.1 placement are arranged vertically. The six curricula have been placed along a continuum horizontally across the page from 'oppositional' at one end, to 'regular', 'compensatory', 'supported', 'modified' and 'alternative' at opposite ends.

Table 8.1 Continuum of educational service options

Placement	Curriculum
Regular school full-time inclusion ——— No support	Regular curriculum 100% (OR Counter-hegemonic curriculum where support is built in to the curriculum)
Regular school inclusion ————— Special education teacher support	Regular curriculum 50–100% Compensatory curriculum (AND/OR) Supported curriculum
Regular school inclusion ————— Part-time resource room	Regular curriculum 50–100% Compensatory curriculum (AND/OR) Supported curriculum
Part-time resource room ————— Regular school inclusion	Regular curriculum 25–50% Compensatory curriculum (AND/OR) Modified curriculum Oppositional curriculum
Full-time resource room in regular school —————	Modified curriculum Alternative curriculum# Oppositional curriculum
Segregated day school ————	Alternative curriculum# Oppositional curriculum
Residential school ———— Full support	Alternative curriculum# Oppositional curriculum

Other curriculum options possible, but unusual in this placement

The MSE can have its own curriculum or the MSE can be viewed as a supportive environment for providing access to other curricula, including the National Curriculum (UK). These ideas are similar to those proposed by Sebba *et al.* (1993). Their curriculum model, based upon the ideas of Ouvry (1991), argued that a student may need aspects of several curricula models, and that the student may move in and out of these, but with a common purpose in terms of desired outcomes. Their model is built around three overlapping circles which represent the National Curriculum, the Developmental Curriculum and the Additional Curriculum (including the therapies). Their argument was neatly reduced to a set of five themes by Sebba (1996). They are

> Theme 1: All pupils have a legal entitlement to a broad and balanced curriculum but this does not ensure access in practice . . .
> Theme 2: The whole curriculum is more than just the National Curriculum and the relationship between the parts of the whole curriculum will need to be flexible enough to cope with changing individual needs . . .

Theme 3: Teaching approaches need to balance group work and individual needs and create greater opportunity for pupil directed learning . . .

Theme 4: Effective management of the whole curriculum must involve parents, professionals and the pupils themselves . . .

Theme 5: Personal and social development, as distinct from traditional views of personal and social education, should permeate throughout the curriculum and ethos of the school. (pp. ix–x)

How the curriculum is developed

There are four main methods that can be employed when developing a curriculum. They are:

1. through direct educator rulings (such as the NC),
2. commercial interests (including textbooks such as this one),
3. opening the process up to subset member input (as discussed in the section on counter-hegemonic curriculum), and
4. critical self-examination and public debate. (Connell 1990)

The MSE curriculum has not yet been subject to sufficient critical self-examination and public debate, nor has it had much subset member input. It will be a sign of its maturity when MSE curricula have been developed by combinations of all four methods.

An outcome-based approach

In the sixties and seventies, curriculum development was inward-looking with education being seen as an input process. The emphasis was on the student gaining experience through a variety of pedagogy. Curriculum development during this period enabled schools to make major improvements in their ability to deal with their increasingly diverse population. The goal was equality of educational opportunity or input.

In the eighties and nineties, a curriculum paradigm shift occurred where the curriculum emphasis turned outwards to student learning outcomes. The driving force behind the curriculum became the need to identify what students actually learn and to examine what impact these learning outcomes have on the economy and the society as a whole. The new goal is equality of educational outcome.

In the outcomes-based approach 'Educational structures and curriculum are regarded as *means* not ends. If they do not do the job they are re-thought' (Willis and Kissane 1997, p. 5).

> It is a very accountable process. The teacher, the school and the system are expected to state what is important for students to learn and to be able to support these assertions with evidence that it has occurred. Such an approach differs from previous orientations as it changes the focus to what is achieved rather than what is provided. (Griffin 1998, p. 9)

This curriculum paradigm shift is particularly pertinent in relation to the MSE where the distinction between means and end has been blurred (see Chapters 1 and 2). There is an ongoing danger that 'what is provided' in the MSE becomes so seductive and engaging for the educator that 'what is achieved' by the student fades into the background or is ignored completely. In the outcome-based approach the educator is the facilitator of learning, using a variety of techniques to help the student learn what he or she 'needs' to learn.

Curriculum design begins with assessment to identify where the student is on a continuum of learning and to identify the most appropriate learning outcomes. The learning outcomes are translated into an intended curriculum which informs the enacted curriculum. Assessment then identifies the match between the learned curriculum and learning outcomes. For students with learning difficulties to achieve measurable learning outcome success there must be effective teaching and learning practices specifically designed to cater to their individual needs. The MSE provides a useful and timely addition to the educator's repertoire of effective teaching and learning practices (see Appendix) thus enabling educators to make closer ties between learning outcomes and the learned curriculum.

In an outcome-based approach the MSE must produce learning outcomes that have 'meaning beyond showing success in school' (Crowther 1998, p. iv). An important focus question of an outcomes-based MSE curriculum is 'How will this learning outcome impact positively on this student when he or she leaves school?' Does this learning outcome make the student more independent? Does this learning outcome extend this student's life choices? If these questions cannot be answered in the positive, then the MSE may not be appropriate for that particular student.

Individualised Education Plan (IEP)

The IEP approach is now used extensively throughout the western world to organise the delivery of appropriate special education services to school-age children. Outside the broad IEP umbrella there are other programmes to address specific needs at other specific stages of the child's development. In early childhood the plan may be called an individual family services plan (IFSP) or an individual developmental plan (IDP). Here the focus is on ensuring that educational services are started early and coordinated with all the other relevant services within an ecological family-orientated perspective. In adolescence an individual transition plan (ITP) can be developed where the focus is on ensuring that the teenager with special needs is adequately prepared for adult community living. All three plans, IEP, IDP and ITP, need to be based on a curriculum which has involved systematic, consultative and constructive processes.

Throughout the world individual education authorities formalise this process in ways which match leglislative requirements. In the UK, a formal Code of Practice ... (DFE 1994) lays down that a continuum of special educational needs (SEN) should be reflected in a continuum of educational services, with the needs of most children being met in mainstream schools, through strong school–parent–child partnerships. A five-stage model, clearly supporting the IEP, has been established to help match the child with disability's SEN to educational provision:

> Stage 1: class or subject teachers identify or register a child's special educational needs and, consulting with the school's SEN coordinator ... take initial action;
> Stage 2: the school's SEN coordinator takes lead responibility for gathering information and for coordinating the child's special educational provision, working with the child's teachers;
> Stage 3: teachers and the SEN coordinator are supported by specialists from outside the school;
> Stage 4: the LEA [local education authority] consider the need for a statutory assessment and, if appropriate, make a multidisciplinary assessment;
> Stage 5: the LEA consider the need for a statement of special educational needs and, if appropriate, make a statement and arrange, monitor and review provision. (p. 3)

The IEP is a written commitment of responsibilities, resources and services involving all relevant educators, the child's parents and, if possible, the child. The IEP can be written using an outcomes-based approach (see text in brackets). Essentially the IEP contains:

- details of child's current level of achievement (document and analyse student's current achievement);
- annual educational goals including short-term objectives (identify learning outcomes);
- anticipated dates and duration of special education services (effective teaching and learning strategies);
- appropriate objective evaluation procedures, with at least an annual review to determine if instructional goals and objectives have been met (assessment of learned curriculum to identify match with learning outcomes).

For a child with special needs, the IEP would delineate whether the MSE was appropriate and, if so, the allocation of time, personnel and resources to be devoted to its use. For example Sailor *et al.* (1993) described an outcomes-based approach to IEP development for Holly, a girl with a severe learning difficulty who was being included in a regular grade two class.

During each activity within the second grade, individual outcomes for Holly were targeted. In some instances the outcomes for Holly related to materials and routines similar to those being used by the other students with a different level of individual performance, and in other instances, the outcomes related to interactions with the other students while engaging in the activities. In some instances, the outcomes were very similar to the outcomes for Holly's nondisabled peers, and in other instances, they were different. When the existing context or strategy provided by the second-grade activities was not facilitative of Holly's IEP goals, alternative activities with second graders were designed or alternative teaching strategies were developed to encompass heterogeneous groups. In a few instances, Holly left to receive her instruction in other integrated environments within the school or in the community but was accompanied by second graders who also benefited from the nonclassroom lesson or activity. (p. 5)

This example shows how, even in a fully-inclusive programme, the MSE could be incorporated using an outcomes-based IEP approach. Holly could attend the MSE once a week and be accompanied by other second grade students who might use the experience as a stimulus for creative writing or as a journal entry.

Assessment in the MSE

Assessment is an essential ingredient of MSE curriculum development and is used to inform all decision-making stages. Prior decision-making stages to MSE use include diagnosis, prognosis, determination of eligibility for special education provision and placement. Ongoing decision-making processes during MSE use are IEP planning, evaluation and review. Assessment is particularly important in a learning-outcomes-driven curriculum.

IEP development, particularly that which relates to the MSE, includes preparation of a comprehensive transdisciplinary statement of the child's current level of achievement. This statement provides an extensive profile of the child's strengths, limitations and most effective learning styles. This information is used to write goals and objectives in the form of learning outcomes. Ongoing assessment procedures enable the team to monitor the IEP over time, to ensure goals and objectives are met and changing needs are being recognised and addressed. Assessment therefore needs to be continuous and integrated.

MSE assessment information comes from each member of the transdisciplinary team and is integrated. The process is multidimensional (and multi- purpose and has multiple domains: cognition, language, socio-emotional aspects, gross and fine motor control, self-care, motivation, social competence, play, temperament, attention, emotional expression, coping behaviour, problem-solving and learning styles).

Assessment information from the child's family usually comes from interviews which can be structured or unstructured. Further assessment information comes from direct observation. Bailey and Wolery (1984) described observation as 'a means of discerning what behaviors are performed by children, under what conditions those behaviors appear, and which stimuli are related to those behaviors' (p. 65). Observation is a particularly useful assessment approach when using the MSE. A third form of assessment information comes from direct assessment. This involves the use of standard tasks which are required using predetermined administration procedures and methods for interpretation. Few standardised tests are currently available for use in the MSE.

Neisworth and Bagnato (1988) identified eight types of assessment measures. Most of these are useful in the MSE. They are:

1. curriculum-based assessment (child displays mastery of objectives within a continuum of objectives);
2. adaptive-to-handicap assessment (content modified to permit alternative sensory or response mode);
3. process assessment (capabilities of children with severe to profound learning difficulties who seem untestable are identified through noting changes in child's reactions – e.g. eye movement, smiling, and inferring understanding);
4. norm-based assessment (child's developmental skills compared to normative group);
5. judgement-based assessment (similar judgements made in different settings by several transdisciplinary team members regarding child's skill or ability);
6. ecological assessment (evaluation focusing on the child's physical, social, physiological development within a range of different environments, MSE, school, home);
7. interactive assessment (evaluation which focuses on the reciprocal nature of child adult interactions, particularly their content and quality);
8. systematic observation (direct observation and recording of behaviour, could involve the use of video recording MSE sessions – suitable for use in the MSE).

Formative evaluation is used to make decisions to modify, change or refine the MSE curriculum part of the IEP implementation. It can also be included to inform summative evaluation regarding the use of the MSE in general. Summative evaluation, that which documents the attainment of programme goals, is used to make decisions regarding whether a particular programme, such as the MSE, should be introduced, terminated or maintained. Both levels of evaluation are vital and need to be ongoing in the MSE.

The curriculum and the MSE

For students who require special education, via the modified, alternative, compensatory or oppositional curricula, the MSE is a useful addition to the teaching armamentarium. The MSE, when used with intelligence and sensitivity, can help to fulfil the goals of making the curriculum broader, more balanced, more relevant, better differentiated, more appropriate (age, level, medium) and able to meet individual student needs. MSE curricular options and details regarding in which chapter these options are covered can be found in Table 10.1 in Chapter 10.

The following two curriculum chapters provide examples of possible MSE approaches in different learning difficulty areas. Particular emphasis has been placed on choosing examples where the goal is to help the student develop a concept of 'who am I' (see Chapters 3 and 6). It is not possible nor desirable to provide didactic information; a cookbook approach with recipes for each major disability group has been eschewed in favour of a broader, more holistic approach.

The suggestions described in this book are merely that – suggestions. It is your responsibility to deconstruct and reconstruct these suggestions to suit the individual needs of your individual students. Likewise it is your responsibility to identify the most appropriate learning outcomes for your students through a range of procedures including collaboration, ongoing examination of the research literature, critical self-examination, conducting own research, being aware of educator rulings, commercial programmes, subset member input, public debate and as Sebba (1996, p. x) urges 'the pupils' themselves.

Chapter 9
Children with a learning difficulty

Introduction

In Chapter 2 the MSE is described as a potentially open-minded space, a multifunctional space able to be used by the child with a learning difficulty for leisure and recreation, for therapy and for education. Transdisciplinary team members can collaborate to develop a curriculum for the child's IEP. An outcomes-based approach to curriculum development helps direct the focus on to the individual child's learning achievements.

Most children receive an appropriate education in the regular classroom via the regular curriculum. Children with learning difficulties often require curriculum modifications, adjustments and accommodations to the regular curriculum in the regular classroom to achieve an appropriate education. However, for children with severe learning difficulties, a more radical approach may be required. Some children have such inflexible learning styles it is extremely difficult to find classroom educational strategies that will enable them to achieve measurable learning outcomes.

The MSE permits members of the transdisciplinary team to collaboratively use interpersonal problem-solving to create a learning environment where the stimuli can be controlled, manipulated, intensified, reduced, presented in isolation or combination, packaged for active or passive interaction, matched to fit the child's motivation, interests, leisure, recreation, therapeutic and educational needs. In short it is an environment designed specifically for an individual child which takes into account everything the transdisciplinary team has discovered about the child and then uses that know-how to construct a learning environment to enable the child to begin the learning process.

This chapter provides accounts of how a child with a severe learning difficulty might be taught to learn how to see using available vision and how to hear using available hearing. (Accounts regarding teaching a child to learn how to use other available senses for learning are outlined in Chapter 10.) The second part of this chapter examines curriculum development using the MSE in relation to six types of learning difficulty:

1. visual impairment,
2. hearing impairment,

3. physical disability,
4. intellectual disability,
5. communication disorder, and
6. behavioural-emotional disorder.

Each learning difficulty is examined in isolation and possible MSE approaches specifically relating to that learning difficulty are identified. MSE curriculum considerations for children with severe to profound multiple learning difficulties are examined in Chapter 10.

Natalie Barraga

Until the sixties it was generally assumed if a child did not automatically learn to see as part of the 'normal' developmental process then that child would never be able to see. Barraga was concerned that some children had potential visual capacity, but were not able to effectively use it. She began to identify ways to help start the 'learning to see' process. She drew clear distinctions (1964) between visual capacity (the ability to see), visual perception (the ability to understand and interpret all visually received information), visual functioning (how available vision is used) and visual efficiency (the ease, comfort and minimum time required to perform a visual task).

Barraga discovered it was possible to improve visual functioning in some children with very low vision. She observed that a child's visual functioning is shaped by 'experiences, motivations, needs and expectations . . . in relation to whatever visual capacity is available to satisfy curiosity and accomplish activities for personal satisfaction' (Barraga 1983, p. 24). Although visual efficiency is often difficult to measure and predict, assessment of visual efficiency greatly assists the educator determine the most appropriate educational methods to teach the child with very low vision how to use available vision more effectively.

Barraga's research showed that a child's visual functioning and efficiency can be developed through carefully planned programmes. The more visual experiences the child has, the more visual pathways to the brain are stimulated, and the greater the repertoire of accumulated visual images and memories that become available for the child to be able to make informed decisions or educated guesses regarding what is being observed. Children with healthy eyes and visual pathways learn to see automatically, spontaneously. The child with low vision, however, needs to be taught to make maximum sense of what ability he or she has. The precise way the child is taught will be influenced by the child's abilities and range of learning difficulties. A child with a severe intellectual disability will need to be taught using different methods from those used with a child with high intellectual functioning.

The work of Barraga has been used to inform the development of other sense abilities: taste, smell, hearing, auditory, tactile, kinaesthetic. For each sense area, the more sense experiences the child actively engages in, the more sense pathways to the brain are stimulated, and the greater the repertoire of accumulated sense images and memories that become available for the child to aid interpretation of the sense information.

Learning to use available vision

Vision is the dominant sense ability for learning. In sighted children about 80 per cent of all learning is thought to be through vision. Even for children with a visual impairment, the more use they are able to make of any available vision the richer the opportunities for learning. Children with very low vision need to be explicitly taught how to interpret and integrate limited vision and the MSE provides a suitable environment for such a programme.

To begin with, a full visual assessment is mandatory and the educator must be provided with detailed reports on the child's visual abilities (see Box 9.1). Assessment may be objective or subjective and needs to be ongoing. It is also worthwhile being aware of possible low vision aids that might be used to help the child see more clearly, such as monoculars, big black felt-tipped pens, closed circuit television.

Visual skill/test	Description
distance visual acuity:	the ability to clearly and sharply discern a distant object
near visual acuity:	the ability to clearly and sharply discern a near object
stereopsis:	the ability to determine relative distance (depth perception); requires coordinated functioning of both eyes
colour vision:	the ability to detect different hues particularly in the red/green range. This is a genetically determined factor more common in boys than girls
heterophoria:	the straightness of the two eyes relative to each other when in their position of rest
accommodative and fusional vergence	The ability of the eyes to maintain focus at near range, and to change focus quickly and accurately
cover test:	a measurement of the degree of imbalance in the relative fixation of each eye
ocular motility:	there are two main types of eye movements, both require the eyes to work together as a team: the first type, saccades, are quick and accurate movements which are used to jump from one object or word to another; the second type, tracking, describes smooth and accurate eye movements used to follow a moving object. Children who lose their place while reading may have poorly developed eye movement skills
near point of convergence:	this is the ability to point or aim both eyes exactly at the same object at the same time. If the eyes do not point precisely at the same object the brain must interpret a slightly different message from each eye which could result in double vision, headaches, tiredness or confusion

Box 9.1 Important visual skills for education (From Alchin and Pagliano 1988) (Reprinted with permission)

Barraga (1974) described a sequence of steps in a 'learning to see' process for children with very low vision. These have been modified and are reinterpreted here as a MSE activity.

Visual stimulation – gaining the child's visual attention

Visual stimulation is a process whereby the child becomes aware of his or her vision. A vital prerequisite is that the child's visual attention must be initially gained before being maintained. This may be a considerable challenge if the child has extremely low vision and has experienced life so far in a blurred and meaningless visual haze. Lack of visual reward results in the child being visually 'switched off'.

The white room MSE provides a visually interesting environment which is designed to be qualitatively different to past visual experiences, a non-threatening blend of lights, colour and movement. Pagliano (1997a) reports on a teacher's story of a ten-year-old female student who had not previously used her vision to any appreciable extent.

> There's this girl who usually keeps her eyes shut . . . . Her name is Janelle. In the [MSE] . . . she has her eyes open all the time watching the other children in the group. The change has been quite dramatic. I think that she's just so fascinated by the other children moving in the room. Perhaps the different changes in light too. She gets such a visual reward from the [MSE] . . . that she keeps her eyes open all the time. (Teacher)

Should the white room MSE elicit no response, the dark room MSE is the next option. The dark room MSE provides the child with much more powerful visual stimulation because of the heightened contrasts (see Chapter 4). However, overstimulation of tenuous visual pathways can be counter-productive, especially in the early stages, and for this reason the white room is better tried initially. Here the goal is to provide just enough visual stimulation to entice the child to want to see. The process could be likened to trying to encourage a snail to come out of its shell. Just the right amount of stimulus and lots of waiting. During this initial stage the visual pathways are hightly vulnerable so the system itself is designed to protect itself. The visual pathways only begin to strengthen through use over time. Too much stimulation initially could result in the child ceasing the visual activity altogether.

Furthermore even talking to a child fully concentrating on a visual activity during this early stage can override and eclipse the newly developing visual pathways to such an extent that the visual interaction ceases to make an impact. Just gaining visual attention, a major breakthrough if a new experience for the child, can be a long process. The MSE can provide the rich rewarding cocoon to encourage this to occur.

Visual stimulation – maintaining the child's visual attention

During the maintenance stage, the child is *visually* encouraged to keep attending to visual stimuli. This requires the educator to identify what is possibly going to be visually appealing to the child, and to keep precise records of observations to help evaluate whether the same visual stimuli remain appealing over time. Visual stimuli could include particular colours, slowly moving lights, flashing lights, UV lights, fluorescent objects, brightly coloured sweets (see Table 4.1), whatever you think might appeal visually to the child. Different stimuli will appeal to different children. At this early stage it is particularly important for the educator to be aware of visual contrast, lighting, positioning of visual stimuli, positioning of the child – particularly the child's head, whether visual images are stationary or moving.

Visual stimulation – doing something with the child's visual attention

Once the child begins to attend to basic visual stimuli with relative ease, the next task is to make the visual stimuli gradually more complex. For example, visual stimuli can be varied by being close to the child, then fading into the distance, stationary then moving clockwise/anticlockwise, smooth then abrupt, slow then fast, directly in front of the child then at an angle. The sequence of visual stimulation may need to evolve over an extended period of time. The educator must make careful observations of the child's looking behaviours in order to build up a detailed knowledge bank of what is appealing to the child and what is inhibiting looking behaviour. Each child will react in different ways and progress is rarely linear. Much repetition is needed to help the child develop a visual memory. Once again the MSE can be a useful tool to facilitate this development.

Awareness of form perception

Form perception is based on a comprehension of shape, contrast, colour, lighting and size. Initial awareness of form begins with the outline, usually a silhouette. Once this level of form recognition has been established, then colour, contrast, light and size can be manipulated to help the child gradually build up a repertoire of meaningful visual memories. The child moves from recognition of solid black forms to recognition of more subtle forms with some internal detail.

Concrete objects that can be viewed and touched simultaneously can be useful at this stage (provided it is the child's choice to engage in two sensory activities, rather than it being an external imposition). The bubble tube is a good example of a simultaneously rewarding visual and tactile experience. Different light colours help to emphasise the shape and visual character of the bubble tube. The vibrations of the bubble tube reinforce its tactile nature. Another example of an interesting visual stimulus that can be felt is the fibre-optic spray.

Naming visual experiences

The next step is the naming of figures, forms and actions and the recognition of them in a wide range of differing circumstances (e.g. near, far, high, low, bright, dull, large, small, in different colours, moving clockwise, anti-clockwise). While the MSE could be used for this, there is no particular advantage to doing so. Subsequent steps are even more sophisticated tasks. They involve the use of vision to achieve visual closure, visual unification and visual organisation. Finally the child needs to engage in visual work in the area of abstract symbology, particularly numbers and letters necessary for the development of visual literacy and numeracy. These visual tasks are best completed in the classroom.

Barraga (1974) identified eight steps to promote the development of visual perceptual skills. These are for the child to:

1. identify likenesses and differences paying particular attention to the object's size, position in space and descriptive details;
2. match two objects by size, colour, shape;
3. sort four items into two categories (size, colour, shape);
4. order items in terms of a defining characteristic such as size;
5. group items by use or by their possible relationship with each other;
6. match names with visual images;
7. recognise shapes, pictures, objects, letters, numbers even though parts are missing;
8. use picture puzzles to promote the integration of parts into the whole.

Obviously once the student is visually functioning at this level, the activities would move outside the dark MSE.

Educational blindness

For children who are educationally blind, no appeal to learning through vision is possible, by definition. Information needs to be transmitted in other ways and therefore emphasis is given to maximising learning through the other senses. Children with low vision can also benefit from these approaches.

Learning to use available hearing

The more use for learning that children with a hearing impairment can make of their limited hearing the better. Ongoing full auditory assessment is mandatory and may be objective or subjective. The educator must be provided with detailed reports on the child's auditory abilities. In addition to the baseline impairment, intercurrent outer and middle ear infections and their sequelae can superimpose negative fluctuations in hearing. Educators need to know how to look after each child's hearing aid and how to connect the FM system to audio visual devices used in the MSE.

The majority of students with hearing impairment have sufficient residual hearing to warrant the use of hearing aids. Hearing aid technology continues to improve (digital aids, filters, better ear moulds, FM) to complement this residual hearing. Research indicates, however, that the mere fitting of a hearing aid is insufficient alone (Ross and Giolas 1978). It is usually necessary to implement a programme that specifically teaches the student how to use his or her hearing more efficiently and effectively.

'Learning to hear' follows similar steps to those developed by Barraga (1974). Auditory stimulation, where the child becomes aware of his or her hearing, can be facilitated in the MSE, especially if the floor is sprung and the room is acoustically sharp. Gaining the child's auditory attention may be difficult, especially if the child has profound hearing loss and has experienced life so far with quietness or slurred and meaningless noise. The ongoing lack of meaningful auditory reward may have resulted in the child remaining aurally inert.

Nielsen's (1994b) resonance board may help the child make a connection between the sounds he or she makes and the sounds he or she hears by linking together sound and vibration. The MSE could be built as a resonating chamber and children could sit or lie on a sprung wooden floor which vibrates with each sound each child makes. The MSE could contain a number of noise-making instruments (horns, whistles, wood blocks, musical instruments) and the child encouraged to experiment. Achieving auditory attention in the child may be a major breakthrough and take a long time to happen.

During the auditory stimulation maintenance stage the child is *aurally* encouraged to attend to auditory stimuli. It could begin with long periods in the MSE listening to music. Speakers can be placed in each corner of the room, at both ceiling and floor levels to encourage interest in sound directionality.

Once the child begins to attend to the auditory stimuli with relative ease then the stimuli may gradually be designed to become more complex. The auditory stimulation may be close to the child, then gradually fade into the distance moving from speaker to speaker, stationary coming from just one speaker then gradually moving clockwise or anticlockwise from speaker to speaker, low in frequency then gradually moving up the frequency scale. This sequence of auditory stimulation may need to evolve over an extended period of time. The educator must make careful observations of the child's auditory attending behaviours in order to build up a detailed knowledge of what is appealing to the child and what is inhibiting listening behaviour. Children need to learn which ear is better at hearing and develop strategies to ensure that they are able to benefit from their hearing in that ear.

Each child will react in idiosyncratic ways, but there will be general similarities as well. Sometimes new stimuli will succeed, other times it may not and the educator may need to go back to previous approaches that proved attractive to the child. During this stage much repetition is needed to help the child begin to develop an auditory memory.

Luetke-Stahlman and Luckner (1991) suggest that auditory skills be divided into four levels:

1. detecting sounds (awareness of the presence of sound),
2. sound discrimination (the ability to differentiate between two sounds),
3. auditory pattern identification (ability to detect and discriminate pattern consisting of more than one sound),
4. comprehension of speech.

To prepare the child for conversational speech, they advocate 'auditory training'.

> Auditory training involves teaching students to *listen* and to make use of their residual hearing. Listening differs to hearing in the degree of understanding and effort involved. Learning to listen occurs when students seek to extract meaning from the acoustic events that surround them all day and every day. Listening takes effort; hearing may not. Auditory training supplements auditory experience, allowing skills that are not learned in a natural way to be presented systematically in a more structured environment. The term auditory training is used to describe numerous teaching methods designed specifically for improving students' auditory speech-perception performance .... Auditory training should include developmental language and speech activities that help the student to
>
> 1. develop a more natural ability to relate and monitor the environment
> 2. obtain a more normal voice quality
> 3. improve speech reception
> 4. improve articulation ... (Luetke-Stahlman and Luckner 1991, p. 201)

Others take a less regimented approach, more responsive to the psyche of the child, with an open goal of improving listening. To this end, the MSE can be designed to create an acoustically malleable learning environment (see Chapter 4 and Table 9.2).

Those children who have no residual hearing at all need help to maximise input through their other senses, particularly the visual.

Children with a visual impairment

Children with a visual impairment fit into three subgroups: educationally blind, partially sighted and visually limited (see Table 9.1). Children who are visually limited do not have a learning difficulty associated with visual impairment because after correction they have adequate functional vision.

Table 9.1 Visual impairment: MSE approaches

Disability	Assessment (learning difficulty)	MSE approaches
Educationally blind – a total lack of functional vision for learning, requires assistance to learn through non-visual means.	*Objective* assessment made by ophthalmologists (eye doctors), optometrists (prescribers of vision aids) – see Box 9.1; Mason 1997.	Tactual, auditory and visual stimulation, involvement in soft play area to develop kinaesthetic and motor skills, development of early skills in orientation and mobility, as a leisure and recreation activity.
Partially sighted/low vision – after correction some functional vision is available for learning, requires assistance to make maximum use of remaining sight and may also require assistance to learn through non-visual means, especially if the child has associated disabilities.	*Subjective* assessment of functional vision by special educators using Aitken and Buultjens' (1992) guidelines (Buultjens 1997). *5 steps – learning to see* • visual stimulation – gaining the child's visual attention • visual stimulation – maintaining the child's visual attention • visual stimulation – doing something with the child's visual attention • awareness of form perception • naming visual experiences	Spatial awareness: ball pool may help child develop early, accurate understanding of body awareness as an object existing in space. Spatial concepts developed, expanded through soft play activities, use of water bed, vibrating cushions, jacuzzi, hanging chair. Massage to teach child selected positional concepts: how to identify positional relationships of body parts, how to move body parts in relationship to one another, how to move body in relationship to objects, how to form object to object relationships (Hill and Hill 1980).
Visually limited – after correction normal functional vision exists for learning. (Pagliano 1998b, p. 388)		

Some children with partial sight, especially those with very low vision, may benefit from being taught via the MSE to use their available vision for learning. Children who are educationally blind, especially those in early childhood, may benefit from the MSE particularly in the areas of tactual, auditory, olfactory and kinaesthetic stimulation. The MSE is useful for development of play concepts, using the soft play areas, and orientation and mobility skills, especially those related to spatial awareness and body awareness. Strategies for teaching children with cortical visual impairment and/or multiple disabilities will be examined in Chapter 10.

Children with a hearing impairment

Children with a hearing impairment fit into the subgroups educationally deaf and hard of hearing. The degree of hearing impairment is further subdivided into mild, moderate, severe and profound. Children who have a mild hearing loss are generally able to function adequately in the regular classroom and are unlikely to use the MSE. Children with moderate, severe or profound hearing loss, especially those in early childhood, may benefit from being taught via the MSE to use their available hearing for learning (see Table 9.2). Strategies for teaching children with cortical hearing impairment and/or multiple disabilities will be examined in Chapter 10.

Table 9.2 Hearing impairment: MSE approaches

Disability	Assessment (learning difficulty)	MSE approaches
Deaf – precludes successful processing of linguistic information through audition, with or without hearing aid. *Hard of hearing* - with use of hearing aid, residual hearing sufficient to enable successful processing of linguistic information through audition. British Association of Teachers of the Deaf list four categories of hearing impairment based on hearing loss of volume: *mild* – less than 40 dB loss (difficulty recognising that person is being addressed); *moderate* – 41 to 70 dB loss (will benefit from hearing aid, difficulty hearing when background noise or speaker some distance away); *severe* – 71 to 95 dB loss (normal conversation extremely difficult); *profound* – greater than 95 dB (normal conversation virtually impossible) (Farrell 1997).	*Objective* – by ENT surgeons, by audiologists (prescribers of hearing aids) using audiometer to assess 1. hearing: volume – sound intensity measured in decibels (dB), 2. frequency – pitch measured in Hertz (Hz), in both ears, aided, unaided. Results plotted on audiogram. Provides details of hearing ability, potential correction, plus indication of types of problems person likely to encounter with conversational speech. Students with measurable auditory skills can do auditory discrimination test. *Subjective* – observation of behavioural of responses of child receiving auditory stimulus.	Encourage auditory development (awareness, sound identification, location, preference, volume). *9 steps – learning to hear:* • auditory stimulation – gaining the child's attention • auditory stimulation – maintaining the child's attention • auditory stimulation – doing something with the child's attention • becoming aware of the way I hear best (through left ear, right ear, with hearing aids on, using FM loop) • becoming aware that sounds can be made within us, by us, around us • becoming aware that sounds have different volume, pitch • becoming aware that sounds come from different directions (identify sound source, near, far, track moving sound, move to track moving sound, to left, to right, up, down) • identifying same and different sounds • identifying families of sounds (animals, transport, musical instruments). Enhance communication through increased awareness of environmental dimensions. To increase all aspects of attention span (initiation, maintenance, productiveness) particularly auditory, visual modes.

Children with a physical disability

Physical disability encompasses four subgroups: mild, moderate, severe and profound. Children with a physical disability may be further described as having associated or multiple disabilities (see Chapter 10). When working with a child with a physical disability, the educator must have a detailed understanding of the child's physical ability as well as physical limitations, in order to be able to design an appropriate environment that matches the individual needs of the child. An important part of the educator's role is to minimise the hardship placed on the student intrinsically by the physical disability, for example, by providing appropriate positioning at particular times during the day.

Positioning needs to be done in ways which are comfortable, helpful to the child's motor development and so as to enhance opportunities for the child to engage in learning. A student who is constantly seeking a position of comfort will find the effort tiring and will have less energy or enthusiasm available to attend to learning tasks. 'Proper positioning alters muscle tone, reduces the negative effects of persistent primitive reflexes, and aligns the head and body for optimal facial orientation, reaching and grasping, and manipulating' (Bagnato and Neisworth 1991, p. 50). Usually positioning occurs under the direction of an occupational therapist and physiotherapist but it is clearly useful for other team members to understand what is involved (Finnie 1975). Apart from regular equipment usually found in the MSE (see Table 4.1) positioning equipment that could be used include corner chairs, side lying devices, wedges and strapping.

Campbell (1993) cautioned those who use adaptive equipment for positioning stating

> . . . equipment does not produce either normalized tone or proper body alignment. Well-selected and well-fitted equipment can only maintain postural tone levels and body alignment.
>
> . . . adaptive equipment maintains body alignment only when well fitted and when the individual has been placed properly in the equipment.
>
> . . . adaptive equipment may not produce the specific results desired for each individual. Teachers, parents and therapists must carefully observe the individual using the equipment over time and in a variety of situations to determine whether or not the desired function is achieved.
>
> . . . Many individuals with dysfunction in posture lack the postural tone necessary to remain in static positions for long periods. Restricting them to one position (even in equipment that fits well and is otherwise comfortable) can produce secondary problems, such as poor circulation, skin ulcerations, muscle tightness, and contractures that lead to deformity. Teachers and parents should ask therapists to specify the length of time the individual can be positioned in equipment. Some individuals can stand or sit comfortably for long periods of time (2 to 3 hours). Other individuals should be repositioned as frequently as every 20 to 30 minutes. (p. 253)

Educators often need to develop a set routine for moving individual children. This could involve a number of the following strategies:

- Inform the child you intend to move him/her.
- Explain where you are moving to and why.
- Make certain the child is ready to move; this may require some massage to attain body alignment or to reduce tone.

- Preparation for lifting could involve moving the child to a seating or standing position.
- Inform the child when you are going to lift him/her.
- Involve the child as much as possible.
- Follow safety recommendations regarding lifting.
- Once the child has been repositioned, inform the child that repositioning had been completed and that the new activity is about to begin.

Table 9.3 Physical disability: MSE approaches

Disability	Assessment (learning difficulty)	MSE approaches
Disabilities of function related to physical skills, such as hand use, body control, mobility, and/or medical conditions, such as loss of strength or stamina (not impairments of vision or hearing) that interfere with school attendance or learning to such an extent that special services are required. *Mild* – independence in meeting physical needs. Potential to improve quality of motor and/or perceptual skills with therapy, without therapy regression likely. *Moderate* – some independence, functional head control, deficits interfere with academic achievement/age-appropriate motor skills. *Severe* – total dependence in meeting physical needs, poor head control, deficits prevent academic achievement/age-appropriate motor skills (McKee *et al.* 1983). *Associated* – when two disabilities present. *Multiple*- when more than two present (see Chapter 10).	*Learning difficulties:* related to processing, motivation, participation. Causes: *Neurological:* cerebral palsy, multiple sclerosis, spina bifida, spinal cord injury. *Musculo-skeletal:* juvenile rheumatoid arthritis, limb deficiency, muscular dystrophy, scoliosis. *Health conditions:* allergies, asthma, cancer, cystic fibrosis, diabetes mellitus, epilepsy, heart problem, haemophilia, sickle cell anemia. *Miscellaneous:* accidents, burns, child abuse. Associated problems: *Hypertonia* – gradual acquired limitation in range of motion, muscle contractures, limited joint mobility, muscle/ligament shortening. *Hypotonia* - muscle weakness particularly in neck and trunk. When severe may require external support to achieve, maintain upright position. Chronic, abnormal positioning can result in joint deformity, muscle atrophy. Levels of paralysis: hemiplegia (arm and leg on same side), quadriplegia (all four limbs), paraplegia (legs only).	Opportunity for affective/emotional development Some physical disabilities seriously limit physical activity, peers inhibited by physical appearance, therefore need to explicitly program for social/affective/emotional development. Stimulation of all senses: tactual, visual, auditory, olfactory, kinaesthetic, taste, somatosensory. Gross motor – maintain, increase child's ability to move about. Fine motor – maintain, increase eye-hand coordination, manual dexterity, switch control. Relaxation–leisure. Facilitation of therapy (physiotherapy) (occupational therapy) (communication therapy) Enhancement of communication (may require augmentative/alternative communication means). Minimisation of challenging behaviours. Development of self-determination – use of switches, cause effect, perseverance. Play. Reasoning, problem-solving, memory skills.

The MSE incorporates many activities appropriate for children with a physical disability, of a variety of ages and severity. These include the ball pool, the water bed, massage, use of switches, facilitation of therapy, relaxation and leisure, affective social/emotional development.

Children with an intellectual disability

Children with an intellectual disability fit into four subgroups: mild, moderate, severe, profound (see Table 9.4). Children with severe to profound intellectual disabilities may benefit considerably from receiving some of their education in the MSE. The MSE is useful in helping to develop skills related to a wide range of curriculum areas:

- leisure and recreation,
- vocational and daily living,
- communication,
- physical development,
- social skills,
- cognitive development,
- functional academics.

(See Chapter 10 for further details regarding working with children with severe to profound multiple disabilities.)

Some skills that could be developed in the MSE for children with severe to profound intellectual disability include:

- stimulation of the senses (e.g. visual fixation, tracking, search);
- hand–eye coordination (e.g. reach, grasp, use equipment);
- identification of objects by sensory characteristic (e.g. smell, shape, colour, location, texture, size, sound);
- spatial relationships, operational causality;
- balance, posture, movement from one position to another, walking;
- gross motor, fine motor;
- looking and imitating behaviour;
- receptive and expressive communication;
- recognition of important signs (e.g. entry, push door, exit, danger);
- play;
- leisure, recreation;
- social skills (e.g. awareness of others, considering others, interaction with others, sharing with others);
- coping with change of routine, design;
- coping with equipment breakdowns;
- use facilities appropriately;
- follow safety procedures.

Table 9.4 Intellectual disability: MSE approaches

Disability	Assessment (learning difficulty)	MSE approaches
Substantial limitations in present functioning. It is characterised by significantly sub-average general intellectual functioning, existing concurrently with related limitations in two or more of the following applicable adaptive skill areas: communication, self-care, home living, social skills, community use, self-direction, health and safety, functional academics, leisure, and work. Mental retardation (intellectual disability) manifests before age 18 (American Association on Mental Retardation 1992).

Students with an intellectual disability develop skills at a slower rate, require more practice, repetition, time; generally have a reduced vocabulary | Significantly sub-average refers to IQ score e.g. WISC >2SD below 100 (i.e. 70) further subdivided into: *mild* 3SD *moderate* 4SD *severe* 5SD *profound* 6SD. Adaptive behaviour measured by tests: Adaptive Behavior Scale (Nihira,*et al.* 1974) Vineland Adaptive Behavior Scale (Sparrow, *et al.* 1984) i.e. curriculum areas (Bowd 1990) focus on basic daily living skills to promote personal independence (use toilet, communicating using gestures)

Curriculum for students with severe/profound intellectual disability: match individual student needs, relevant, age-appropriate, encourage full participation, whole of life, transdisciplinary, variety of resources, support services, learning environments, slow pace down | **Structure learning environment** to maximise student's experiences of success, to enable students to learn by doing, to encourage open-ended problem-solving, to span multiple subject areas. Curriculum areas related to MSE – *Communication:* awareness of self/others; attending (visual/auditory); listening; recognising symbols/ names; naming MSE equipment/activities; imitating sounds/words; making choices; Yes/No; indicating personal needs; same/different; requesting help; terminating task. *Mathematics:* counting; sequencing *Science:* colour. *Health and physical education:* hydrotherapy; sitting skills; standing; transfer from one activity to another; walking; ball games; fitness; dancing; trampoline; body awareness; sense development; body parts. *Life skills:* friendships; turn-taking; appropriate behaviours; self-confidence; manners; recognising/responding to others. *The Arts:* using play equipment; tv, radio, video, computer; music. *Technology:* switch (cause/effect) – see above, leisure planning using MSE. |

Children with a communication disorder

Children with a communication disorder fit into two subgroups: those with language disorders and those with speech disorders (see Table 9.5). Children with a severe communication disorder of whichever kind are unable to produce or use speech. Such children must therefore use an augmentative or alternative form of communication. The MSE may be particularly useful in early childhood to help support the child's emerging communication skills. The MSE provides increased opportunity for:

- joint child adult attention on an activity
- turn-taking (interaction, visual – eye gaze, tactile, auditory, vocalisation, verbal)
- contingent responsiveness (quick, accurate, meaningful adult response to child's communicative attempt)

- positive affection (smiling, gentle touch, physical presence, physical stimulation such as rocking, massage, blowing, singing). (Kaiser 1993; Vitagliano 1988)

Goossens *et al.* (1994) identified seven barriers to communication development for children with a severe communication disorder.

1. A lack of clarity of intent because of the frequently observed tendency to use imprecise forms of communication (e.g. vocalisations, eye pointing, facial expressions) rather than more precise forms (e.g. picture communication symbols, Compic, signs such as Makaton, Signed English, British Sign Language, Auslan, Amslan).
2. The more precise forms of communication are used mainly in response to teacher-initiated questions rather than spontaneously.
3. Any communication so structured that it is limited in range and function (particularly in relation to choice).
4. Any communication which is limited to requiring yes/no answers.
5. Communication which is dominated by the educator rather than being an interchange.
6. Communication conducted by adult who fills conversational space, thereby implicitly giving the child the message that an answer is not really expected.
7. Little opportunity for communication with peers possible as overwhelming majority of communication is with adults.

Barriers can be reduced if careful attention is given to the way the MSE is used, such that successful communication is linked with an obvious impact on the child's environment.

Goossens *et al.* (1994) designed a facilator vest which has a Velcro-fastened communication display of Compic or picture communication symbols on the front. Vests can be worn by both adults and children. A child's vest could be as simple as an armband to indicate that the child wishes to communicate or it could be as comprehensive as that worn by the adult. Symbols are chosen after careful analysis of the child's programme to incorporate humour, to include a range of different parts of speech and different language functions. Being Velcro-fastened, symbols are easily removed and replaced when appropriate. Two-way flowing communication can be encouraged through the use of scripting, where the adult models sentence construction, uses symbols to clarify ideas, extend vocabulary and organise thoughts. Modelling the use of symbols through scripting helps to stimulate language, facilitate comprehension and augment communication. Symbols help to establish routine and build anticipation and expectation. This method enables children to:

- ask questions,
- learn comparison skills and classification skills,
- recall information,

Table 9.5 Communication disorders: MSE approaches

Disability	Assessment (learning difficulty)	MSE approaches
Faulty message transmission/perception which places individual in economic, social, learning disadvantage, negative impact on emotional growth Two types: *Language disorders –* deviance in communication code 1. Absence of language (no recognisable receptive, expressive language) 2. Delayed language (acquired at later point in time, slower than normal) 3. Interrupted language (partial loss of language ability) 4. Qualitative disorders (bizarre or meaningless language); *Speech disorders –* Problems in production of intelligible oral language 1. Absence of speech (total lack of intelligible speech) 2. Articulation disorders (errors, distortions in the way speech sounds made) 3. Voice disorders (deviations in pitch, loudness, resonance, voice quality) 4. Fluency disorders (problems in the rhythm, timing, uninterrupted connecting of sounds, phrases) (Kneedler *et al.* 1984, p. 146; Pagliano 1997b)	Assessment – comparison with normal development. If problem suspected child referred. Assessment usually conducted by speech language pathologist/communication therapist. Assessment follows • discussing with the referral agent what the problem seems to be • interviewing caregivers, associated people, child • observing child (variety of settings, tasks, times, people) • sampling communicating behaviour for detailed language analysis • formally testing child. A report is written. *Severe communication impairment:* unable to produce/use intelligible speech, must rely on augmentative (supplemental), alternative methods *Unaided communication systems:* facial expressions, signing, gestures, body language *Aided communication systems:* non-electronic assistive devices, portable dedicated communication devices, computer-based communication systems (Bigge 1991)	Opportunity for affective, emotional development Stimulation of all senses, particularly visual, auditory, tactual, kinaesthetic. Awareness of self, others; attending, listening, recognising symbols, names, making choices, use of yes/no box, indicating personal needs, preferences, same/different, requesting help, change, terminating task. Development of gross motor, fine motor skills. Enhance communication through increased awareness of environmental dimensions. Facilitation of therapy, use of switches (particularly therapies directly related to development of communication skills). To increase all aspects of attention span (initiation, maintenance, productiveness) particularly auditory and visual modes. Development of self-determination skills. Friendship, turn-taking, waiting skills, recognising, responding to others. Leisure and recreation (socialisation, communication).

- build self-esteem (emotionally/physically),
- accept responsibility,
- learn about social rules/cooperation,
- become aware of others (especially peers),
- assist others and understand their needs.

Children with an emotional/behavioural disorder

Definitions regarding emotional/behavioural disorders differ throughout the world. Most are vague and rely heavily on subjective opinion which makes decision making and curriculum planning difficult if only the teacher is involved. It is best to establish a transdiciplinary team where particular members are targeted for their specialist skills.

Children with an emotional/behavioural disorder may fit into four subgroups: conduct disorder, socialised aggression, anxiety-withdrawal, immaturity (Kneedler *et al.* 1984, see Table 9.6). Farrell (1997) used a three subgroup model consisting of:

1. neurotic (anxiety, phobia, obsessive/compulsive, avoidance/withdrawn, hypochondria, hysteria, depression),
2. psychotic (schizophrenia, dementia, toxic confusional/delirious, reactive psychosis), and
3. antisocial (conduct disorder).

Whatever the grouping, three overriding factors determine whether the child has an emotional/behavioural disorder. They are:

- Is the problem chronic (i.e. long standing)?
- Is the problem severe?
- Does the problem cause the child to experience learning difficulties in school?

In order for the child with an emotional/behavioural disorder to receive an appropriate education, modifications, adjustments and/or accommodations must be made to the curriculum.

Children who are emotionally/behaviourally disturbed, especially those in early childhood, may benefit from the MSE, particularly in the areas of tactual, auditory, olfactory and kinaesthetic stimulation. The MSE could be useful for development of play concepts.

Conclusion

In Chapter 1 it was argued that an educational definition of the MSE begins with the individual child. The value of the MSE as an educational tool

Table 9.6 Behavioural/emotional disorder: MSE approaches

Disability	Assessment (learning difficulty)	MSE approaches
Individual exhibits one or more following characteristics: 1. inability to learn, not explained by intellectual, sensory or health factors 2. inability to build or maintain satisfactory relationships with peers or teachers 3. inappropriate types of behaviour or feelings under normal circumstances 4. general pervasive mood of unhappiness or depression 5. tendency to develop physical symptoms or fears associated with personal or school problems 6. autistic 7. socially maladjusted - which • occur over extended period • occur to marked degree • adversely affect educational performance (Bower 1989). Classification: *Conduct disorder* – disobedient, defiant, disruptive, assaultive, impertinent *Anxiety-withdrawal* – hypersensitive, self-conscious, depressed, lacks self-confidence, tense *Socialised aggression* – loyal to delinquent friends, steals in company with others, truant from school *Immaturity* – short attention span, messy, clumsy, fails to finish things, lacks initiative. (Kneedler *et al.* 1984, p. 116) Programmes designed to suit individual needs with ongoing monitoring and review.	Information from parent interviews, standardised tests, behaviour observations, self-reports, peer reports, teacher ratings, anything to contribute to total picture of student's feelings, behaviours, experiences. Six theories inform cause/educational approach: 1. *Behavioural* – faulty reinforcement, inappropriate learning therefore rearrange environmental events 2. *Biological* – genetic, neurological, biochemical factors therefore change in physiology 3. *Ecological* – poor interaction of the child with the ecosystem, therefore change nature of interaction between child and environment 4. *Psychoanalytical* – unresolved psychic conflicts due to imbalance of personality structures (id, ego, superego) or faulty passage through developmental stages (oral, anal, phallic) therefore help child act/talk out unconscious conflicts 5. *Psychoeducational* – inner conflict cycle that includes child's personality structure, emotional reactions, environmental events, therefore create trust, accept feelings, teach academics 6. *Humanistic* – not in touch with own feelings, regular educational setting inappropriate, therefore provide treatment in more personalised setting where teacher more non-directive (Kauffman 1989). Mix and match approaches to suit individual child's needs.	Transdisciplinary team collaboration valuable, may need input from general practitioner (if seizures involved), psychologist, psychiatrist, be aware of child's possible difficulties in adapting to new people, new environments, new approaches, gently introduce each component of programme, sensory stimulation especially touch, respect individual's personal space, privacy, be responsive to child's preferences, allow child to lead, set pace, share, match goals to needs, keep precise measurements, identify possible causes or reasons, conduct functional analysis, monitor and review (see Chapter 2, Henning 1994). Provide options, allow student to choose favourite area, activity, length of time. Emphasis on effective communication. Relaxation, stimulation. Building relationships with carer, educator, peers. Emphasis on remaining actively engaged in stimulating and enjoyable activities that develop in complexity. Possible goals: learning to cope with anxiety, develop feelings of self-worth, learn to accept reasonable guidance and direction, develop behaviour more likely to be accepted by others, develop realistic objectives, effective work habits, positive attitudes. Do not place children who reject one another together. Be consistent, reward success do not punish failure.

therefore depends upon it being meaningful to the child in positive ways. In Chapter 8 this theme was further developed to emphasise that, when using an outcomes-based approach, educational structures and curriculum involving the MSE are simply means to an end – not the end in itself. If educators are not able to demonstrate success, then a decision must be made as to whether the MSE is a suitable option for that particular child, and, if so, on what grounds.

In Chapter 8 a range of curriculum types and assessment procedures were identified that could be used to inform such decision-making. When working with children with severe learning difficulties, success must be directly related to the individual needs of individual children. For example, for children with deteriorating conditions, success may simply mean maintenance of present skills, be gauged by levels of observable enjoyment such as the number of smiles per session or even the reduction in the amount of time spent crying.

In Chapter 9 a wide range of suggestions are made regarding possible uses of the MSE with children with particular learning difficulties. Each child's MSE programme must be based on informed decisions involving:

- all members of the transdisciplinary team
- detailed information of the child's disability
- information detailing the impact the disability has on learning
- full assessment of the child's current level of achievement
- detailed information regarding what the child needs to learn, stated in outcomes
- an individually designed programme which is outcomes based, involves ongoing evaluation and regular review.

Curriculum considerations relating to teaching children with severe to profound multiple learning difficulties using the MSE will be examined in Chapter 10.

Chapter 10

Children with severe/profound multiple learning difficulties

Introduction

Children with severe/profound multiple learning difficulties may exhibit physical, sensory and/or intellectual impairments in addition to challenging behaviour, communication problems and mobility restriction. Nielsen (1979) suggested that learning difficulties multiply, rather than sum, with each different disability; for example the difficulties associated with blindness multiply with those associated with physical disability. Providing an appropriate education for children with severe/profound multiple learning difficulties is therefore an enormously challenging endeavour.

In recent years the MSE has emerged as one of a number of different innovative responses educators have explored in their attempt to more effectively meet this challenge. The ways in which educators have been using the MSE when working with children with severe multiple disabilities are still largely uncatalogued. The intention behind this book is to develop a rationale to enable educators to organise and analyse the disparate practices that are in use.

A bridge to inclusion

This rationale for the MSE has been built on eight underlying themes. They are:

1. An educational definition of the MSE must begin with the individual child (see Chapter 1). The MSE is only of value if it is meaningful and of value to that child.
2. The challenge of providing an appropriate education for the individual child with severe/profound multiple learning difficulties is too complicated and demanding for teachers alone. As Farrell (1997) observed, the 'range and complexity of these difficulties require the involvement of various professionals such as teachers and therapists and close working relationships with parents' (p. 127). A transdisciplinary team effort is required (see Chapter 5).

The term transdisciplinary implies that the team, possibly comprising therapists, teachers, teacher aides and parents, uses collaboration at a primary level . . . . This is in contrast to the term multidisciplinary, which implies that the collaboration is at a secondary level with stakeholders working at a primary level within their own discipline rather than co-operatively across disciplines. (Pagliano 1998a, p. 106)

3. There are two different types of MSEs (see Chapter 2). The 'single-minded' space is constructed for a specific purpose, namely leisure and recreation, therapy, or education and is used in rigid ways by workers from a single discipline. The 'open-minded' space is designed and constructed for multifunctional uses by the transdisciplinary team. Transdisciplinary use of the MSE changes the nature of the learning environment. It can be used for leisure, therapy, education or all three, depending on the needs and wishes of the individual child.

4. An outcomes-based approach to curriculum planning supports trans-disciplinary collaboration because it provides a common achievable goal (see Chapters 5 and 8). Furthermore an outcomes-based approach accentuates the distinction between means and end. In an outcomes-based approach the questions are: 'What has the student actually achieved?' and 'How can this achievement be justified in terms of the standards of an appropriate education?'

5. The open-minded MSE promotes inclusion because it encourages inde-pendence and sharing (see Chapter 2). For many individuals with severe/profound multiple learning difficulties, the MSE may be one of the few environments available to that individual where she or he is able to function at anywhere near an independent level. When used effec-tively, therefore, not only may the MSE have profound effects on the student's learning and life quality, it may also be an important bridge to inclusion. When children are able to function at a more independent level and have fun, they are more likely to interact socially. As one therapist at Mundingburra Special School argued 'They're at their best in the S[MSE]' (p. 78).

If parents and nondisabled brothers and sisters [and peers] see the children happy, laughing and relaxed, as they so often are in the S [MSE], they're going to relate to them more than if they see them cranky, throwing their arms and legs around, dribbling and angry. Unfortunately that's the way they usually are when they see them in the outside world. (Therapist, quoted in Pagliano 1997a, p. 79)

6. A combination of pedagogical approaches in the MSE are required to achieve enhanced learning outcomes for students with severe/profound multiple learning difficulties (see Chapter 9). These pedagogical approaches will be explored further in this chapter.

7. The MSE is just one part of the student's total learning environment. The MSE provides new opportunities for learning that otherwise would be outside the student's experiences. Furthermore, the MSE can be used to complement and enhance the whole curriculum (see Chapter 8).

8. The overriding theme of this book has been to employ a targeted eclectic flexibility through the purposeful adjustment and readjustment of a wide range of MSE continua in direct response to the perceived needs of the child (see Appendix). In the open-minded MSE there is a process of continuous change, where the emphasis is on each child and the approaches used are the fusion of a unique set of multiple, diverse forces at a particular time and in a particular location. An example of a unique set of forces coming together is provided in the story 'Adventure teaching in the MSE' told in Box 10.1. Here the author makes no attempt to make generalisations. The experience only has 'pertinence commensurate to context . . . which can change as context changes' (Webber 1995, p. 440).

Assessment

MSE curriculum development begins with assessment of the individual student's learning and life quality. Assessment must be individualised, ongoing and be conducted by all transdisciplinary team members, working collaboratively in a wide range of contexts over extended periods of time, in order to identify the child's strengths, interests, aptitudes and achievements. Team members decide which assessment will be conducted (e.g. mobility, daily living skills, communication, social interactions, community skills), who will conduct it, who will interpret results and how results will be translated into programme priorities, learning outcomes and pedagogical approaches.

Assessment choices will be influenced by the purpose of the assessment and the underlying philosophy. Assessment may follow a developmental approach, an adaptive behaviour approach, an environmental/ecological approach or a synergistic combination of all three.

The developmental approach

A developmental, or bottom–up approach consists of determining skills an individual would be expected to achieve at a particular age, based on comparison with the normal sequence of development. Instruction follows the path of normal development. Using a developmental approach is attractive because developmental checklist items are easily observed and the list provides direction for future skills that may be taught in the MSE.

Nine 10-to-14-year-old children accompanied by nine adults were transferred from wheelchairs to comfortable floor positions. A loud speaker announced from the darkness 'Citizens of earth, we have come to invade your planet'. While music from 'War of the Worlds' played, Simon the 'adventure teacher' instructed the children to steer their space craft. They were rolled to their left, to their right and propped forward in time with the music. With the words 'flares spurting out from Mars' the children were rolled onto their stomachs. They strained to raise their heads for a better view of two newly-lit sparklers. Audible 'aahs' indicated they had achieved success. Next the children were rolled onto their backs and propped forward to watch the neonate scene from '2001: A Space Odyssey'. This was followed by the UFO landing scene from 'Close Encounters of the Third Kind'. During this scene they were handed cardboard cylinder field glasses (binoculars) and told to watch the invasion of earth.

White noise flooded the room, and toy helmets, ray guns and sci-fi equipment were distributed. The children watched a shadow play, enactment of an 'alien' shooting his ray gun at the 'earthlings'. The earthlings all had hold of their ray guns and were doing their best to shoot the alien. Vocalisations increased significantly. The alien was clearly in trouble. 'You have no hope', the earthlings were told. Without warning, the teacher lurched from behind the sheet holding a grotesque alien doll. 'I have escaped', he called, invading each child's personal body space to confront them face to face. There were squeals of delight! 'Quick, we need to leave this planet'. All earthlings were given fibre-optic torch 'space wands' to control their space ship's progress through hyperspace. The pilots steered their craft up and down, left and right. During this sequence I saw nine children with severe and multiple disabilities firmly holding their space wands, some with appropriate hand–eye coordination, some with appropriate vocalisations, all completely immersed in the action.

'We are coming in for a landing', the adventure teacher announced. The children rocked from side to side as they saw the space ship approach the planet on the monitors. 'There is a lot of space traffic and we have been placed in a holding pattern', the speaker reported. 'Turn off your space wands and settle back for some musical entertainment.' Each child was handed a percussion instrument and David Bowie appeared on the monitors singing 'Major Tom'. Many children were attempting to independently keep the beat and some were vocalising in tune. 'Ladies and gentlemen you are coming in to land. Take up your light swords and prepare to do battle to the death.' The monitors switched to the duel scene in 'Star Wars'. The children were encouraged to become aware of their neighbours and two pairs actively 'engaged in battle' using their space wands. There was more shadow play, this time with Darth Vader, their enemy behind the screen. There was another confronting face-to-face meeting with Darth Vader's friend the alien, followed by sudden total darkness.

'A special morning tea will be served in honour of your victory', the speaker announced. The serving of a meal sequence from '2001: A Space Odyssey' was shown as the adventure drew to a close. The age-appropriate story adventure had been made more exciting by taking place in the MSE. Teachers were genuinely surprised by their student's involvement. 'She really responded. Her eyes opened wide and she laughed. She vocalised at the fibre optics. She stretched out of the beanbag. She visually tracked. She enjoyed the physical contact. She had a really good time.' A second reported his student had 'increased his purposeful head movements and touched the fibre-optic spray' while a third concluded, 'Sandy got very excited when Darth Vader was behind the screen. She fired her gun at him. That was the high point for her.'

Box 10.1 Adventure teaching in the MSE (abridged from Pagliano 1997a, pp. 83–86)

Dale's (1990) stimulation guide is a good example of a developmental approach. His guide provides comprehensive checklists for eight domains:

1. locomotion,
2. occupational,
3. personal/social development,
4. dressing,
5. feeding,
6. washing and bathing,
7. toileting,
8. communication and language
(see 'Normal age levels of development table', Dale 1990, p. 184).

The developmental approach has been criticised because it is built on the assumption that normal development is relevant to the needs of children with disabilities. However the more severe and multiple the disabilities, the more this simplistic assumption must be called into question. Many skills taught when following a developmental scale are neither functionally appropriate nor age-appropriate. The slavish adherence to the developmental approach may result in skills being taught in isolation from each other and from the environment in which the child will be living. Such skills, even if acquired, are unlikely to be maintained over time. A second problem occurs if an assumption is made that certain developmental skills are prerequisites for more advanced skills. The child may be locked into a learning sequence that is neither achievable nor desirable. White (1985) observed, for example, that although head control is necessary for walking, it is not essential for operating a motorised wheelchair.

It is therefore vitally important members of the transdisciplinary team view the developmental approach from both micro (narrowly focused on behaviour within a single domain) and macro (broadly focused on whole of life issues for that individual) perspectives. This enables team members to maintain a much more critical and insightful overview of the child's learning outcomes.

Bozic (1997b) argued that awareness of the child's developmental level helps us to chart further learning outcomes. He explains: 'If we are considering developing a child's use of his or her visual skills in a multi-sensory room for instance, we might ask: what is the child's current repertoire of visual abilities?' (p. 327). When planning takes into account the use of 'Vygotsky's (1978) concept of the zone of proximal development' (ZPD)' (p. 327), the developmental assessment takes on more complex proportions.

> Vygotsky claimed that there are two levels that one should be interested in when assessing a learner's abilities in any domain:
> 1. the learner's actual level of development, that is, what the learner can achieve alone;

2. the learner's potential level of development, that is, what the learner can currently achieve with the help of others.

It is the space between a learner's actual and potential level of development which Vygotsky called the ZPD .... Instruction should aim to place the child into situations just beyond what they can already achieve alone, but no higher than what they can reasonably achieve with the support of others. With successful learning the level of actual development will then shift into what is currently defined as the ZPD, and the level of potential development will rise into new uncharted territory.

What then is the effect of educational technology on learners with multiple disabilities and a visual impairment? Although computers and multi-sensory rooms did not exist in Vygotsky's day (the 1920s and early 1930s), he certainly believed that any kind of tool has the power to extend human potential. It can then be assumed that with the help of technology, as well as a teacher [and transdisciplinary team members], a child may be able to achieve more than he or she would with only the teacher for support. (pp. 337–38)

The MSE and microcomputers can therefore be used by the transdisciplinary team to create optimal conditions, potentially enabling the child to perform at levels beyond that of actual development.

The MSE can be designed in ways that provide scaffolds for learning where the child is able to perform at higher levels than would be possible outside the MSE. Based on observations made within the MSE it may be possible for the educator to design augmentative approaches that can be employed to support the child's higher level functioning in environments outside the MSE (e.g. LaGrow et al. 1998 found that for children with low vision when compared with white light and white stimuli, 'orange stimuli viewed under black light resulted in the best performance overall and was the most preferred condition', p. 313). If regular classrooms are to become more inclusive in their 'contexts for instruction' beyond those 'referenced to the student's same-age peers' (Sailor et al. 1993, p. 17), in line with a counter-hegemonic approach there will need to be new designs emerging in the regular classroom that match the learning needs of children with severe/profound multiple learning difficulties (see Chapter 8). Some of these designs could well come from the MSE (see Chapter 12).

The adaptive behaviour approach

Adaptive behaviour approaches involve measuring skills using checklists (e.g. the Vineland Adaptive Behavior Scale in Sparrow et al. 1984). These skills fit into a number of domains of independent functioning such as:

- physical development,
- economic activity,

- language,
- numbers,
- time,
- domestic,
- vocational,
- self-direction,
- responsibility, and
- socialisation.

The focus when measuring adaptive behaviour is to identify behaviours that will positively impact on the individual's independent functioning in society. Grossman (1983) defined adaptive behaviour as the 'degree with which individuals meet the standards of personal independence and social responsibility expected for age and cultural group' (p. 1).

The adaptive behaviour approach has been criticised because it is vaguely defined, difficult to measure, often requires subjective interpretation, is difficult to clearly differentiate from intelligence and changes with age (Frankenberger and Harper 1988). Still there is much to recommend the careful observation of the child with severe/profound multiple learning difficulties' adaptive behaviour when using the MSE. Luciano (1994) explains

> Observing how the child adapts to new settings and circumstances will shed light on the child's flexibility as well as on his or her tendency to compensate for weaknesses with strengths. This is particularly true in young children with specific disabilities who are adopting alternative means of exploring and interacting with the environment. For example, a child with visual impairment relies more heavily on tactile and auditory cues in his or her contact with objects and people in the environment. If hearing impaired, a child relies on visual cues and physical prompts in order to perform. Movement disabilities, gross or fine in nature, greatly impede a child's free exploration of the surroundings and manipulation of objects.
>
> Noting how the child deals with each situation is important: Does the child ask for assistance? Does the child request that an object be brought to him or her? Does he or she seem to give up trying to obtain it? The child may have established adaptive ways of moving, grasping, and problem-solving. It is essential to provide ample time and opportunity for the child to achieve his or her goal. (p. 36)

The MSE provides an ideal environment to provide the child with new opportunities to encourage the development of adaptive skills. It also provides an excellent environment for educators to be able to make detailed and ongoing observations of the child's skills of adaptive behavious and to plan appropriate learning outcomes.

The environmental/ecological approach

An environmental/ecological approach consists of a top–down approach where, within a range of adult domains, requisite skills for independent adult functioning are identified. An advantage of using a functional approach is the increased likelihood that skills learnt will be used and therefore naturally maintained. 'Since learning is slow and skills loss through disuse is predictable for students with disabilities, target skills that meet the criterion of functionality can facilitate good conditions for skill retention' (Brown and Snell 1993, p. 75). Other advantages are that an environmental approach is easily individualised, flexible, and responsive. One domain of adult functioning that has particular application to the MSE is leisure.

> Assessing environments helps determine whether they facilitate or hinder children's development. Teachers and examiners need to be aware of the complexities of environmental assessments, appreciate the dynamic and interactive nature of environments, and be familiar with a variety of assessment strategies. Information from ecological assessment has important implications with regard to a student's achievement. Information from an environmental assessment is useful when planning and implementing environmental changes. (Bondurant-Utz 1994, p. 197)

Brown *et al.* (1979) described five phases of the ecological inventory process that could be used with the MSE. They are:

1. identify curriculum domains (e.g. leisure);
2. identify and survey current and future environments (e.g. leisure environments);
3. divide environments into sub-environments (e.g. MSE);
4. inventory sub-environments for relevant activities performed there (e.g. see Table 9.1);
5. determine skills required for performance of these activities (see Box 10.1).

Neisworth and Bagnato (1988) listed four basic ecological assessment guidelines:

1. family is an important partner in process;
2. assessments focus on naturalistic observations of child's behaviours in routine interactions;
3. nondiscriminatory assessment instruments (re child's cultural background, economic status, family value system);
4. assessment plan for next most probable placement.

A combined approach to assessment

Assessment to inform curriculum development that employs a synergistic combination of the developmental approach, adaptive behaviour approach and environmental/ecological approach is likely to provide the trans-disciplinary team with a wider range of curriculum options to address the complexity of learning difficulties than that which would be available if only one approach were to be followed. Furthermore the combined approach makes it possible to take advantage of the best a single approach has to offer while recognising and making allowances for the kind of limitations associated with that approach.

Identifying long-term objectives and short-term goals

The transdisciplinary team uses the assessment information to make decisions regarding desired learning outcomes to be achieved in the MSE. Table 10.1 provides a summary of some MSE curricular options that could be used with a student with severe/profound multiple learning difficulties. Many of these options have already been described in detail in other parts of this book.

If a child is so disabled that he or she will only learn a few skills during the course of time spent at school, it makes sense to identify and teach those skills that relate directly to promoting independent adult functioning and self-determination. Transdisciplinary team members continue to observe and record the child's preferences, aversions, interests and needs throughout the entire time the MSE is being used. This provides the team with information that aids the development of a wider ecological/environmental inventory (school, home, community). This information further assists transdisciplinary team members to:

- plan and implement MSE activities to take account of child's preferences, aversions, interests, needs;
- ensure activities are age- and level-appropriate;
- become increasingly more aware of the child's preferences, aversions, interests, needs and how to steer these in more level- and age-appropriate directions;
- identify ways to help the child become more aware of own preferences, aversions, interests, needs;
- refine ways to respond more appropriately to the child's stated wishes and desires;
- challenge the child to become more actively involved in the learning process through self-direction.

An example of a MSE programme can be found in Box 10.2. This programme is used at Mundingburra Special School with children with severe/profound multiple learning difficulties. The programme includes a rationale, a statement of beliefs, goals, objectives, teaching strategies, evaluation techniques and eight key competences.

Table 10.1 MSE curricular options (adapted from Pagliano 1997a, pp. 86-7)

Curriculum area	Objective (learning outcome)	See Chapter
Opportunity for affective/ emotional development	• to promote satisfaction with life (there will be a measurable increase in the number of times the child smiles, a decrease in the number of times the child cries)	6
	• to increase quality of life (there will be a measurable increase in the number, range and types of behaviours the child engages in/displays, both actively, passively)	6
	• to develop a sense of 'who am I' (child demonstrates awareness of own needs, interests, abilities – sets own goals; initiates risky actions; achieves intermediate success; takes responsibility for positive and negative results; revises goals; child influences facilitator's behaviour to ensure activity matches personal needs, interests, abilities)	3, 6
Stimulation for all senses: • tactual • visual • auditory • olfactory • kinaesthetic • taste • somatosensory	• to increase all aspects of attention span (initiation, maintenance and productiveness)	3
	• to increase stimulus tolerance or to reduce defensiveness (all senses, especially tactual)	
	• to encourage visual development (visual awareness, focusing, eye tracking, visual identification, preference)	9
	• to encourage auditory development (awareness, sound identification, location, preference, volume)	9
	• to encourage olfactory development (smell identification, preference, aromatherapy)	
	• to encourage tactile development (tactile awareness, touch identification, preference, massage)	
	• to encourage kinaesthetic development (movement awareness, preference, response to pressure and weight, movement from one activity to another, movement to manipulate activity)	
	• perceptual motor coordination (hand–eye coordination)	
Relaxation	• independent enjoyment of age-appropriate leisure options within an atmosphere of trust, free from pressure	2
Facilitation of therapy (physiotherapy)	• massage increases mobility by maximising joint range and by reducing tone	5
	• ball pool enables the child to find most comfortable body position, thus minimising pain	
(occupational therapy)	• develop fine motor skills associated with using switches, using utensils, dressing, develop increased tolerance of textures	5
(communication therapy)	(see below)	5
Enhancement of communication	• awareness of self	3
	• ability to communicate (pitch, pace, pause, emphasis, volume, stress, vocalisations)	9
	• sign	
	• awareness of activities, choice, preference	
	• awareness of peers, staff, caregivers, family, friends, others	
	• nominating choice	
	• nominating change	
	• expressing feelings, pleasure, displeasure	
	• initiating contact with others, sharing, developing relationships	
	• terminating communication, activity, MSE session	

Table 10.1 *continued*

Curriculum area	Objective (learning outcome)	See Chapter
Minimisation of challenging behaviours	• by increasing appropriate vocalisations • by increasing appropriate behaviour • by decreasing inappropriate self-stimulatory or self-abusive behaviour	2 9
Development of self-determination	• through concepts of ownership, associations, memory and choice, use of switches, cause and effect, perseverence	6 4
Play	• following the child's lead • modelling • solitary play, parallel play, functional–manipulative play, symbolic play, dramatic play, cooperative play	3

Rationale
Provide people who have sensory and learning difficulties with appropriate relaxation and leisure facilities through pleasurable sensory experiences generated in an atmosphere of trust and relaxation.

Beliefs
Everyone needs stimulation. People who have special needs also have the right to appropriate stimulation through sensory experiences that are arranged to stimulate the primary senses without the need for intellectual activity.

Goals
• to provide students with an age-appropriate leisure option (school, post-school access)
• to provide independent enjoyment of the MSE free from pressure
• to provide parents/caregivers with a 'special place' where they can relax and interact with their child. Individual student's preferences may give parents or caregivers incentive to use some of the displays in their home environment: improvement to quality of life
• to stimulate all senses, and desensitise those who are tactile-defensive
• to provide therapeutic massage aimed to maximise joint range and muscle tone
• to provide students with low vision maximum stimulation to encourage focusing, eye tracking and increased attention span to task
• to provide students with choices regarding MSE activities and a sense of ownership regarding the room
• to use the MSE in creative programming combining with other areas of the programme: Conductive Education; relationship play
• to use the MSE to minimise challenging behaviours through:
  – positive reinforcement of good behaviours
  – distraction from self-stimulatory or self-abusive behaviours
  – increase in appropriate vocalisations.

Objectives
• to provide an environment for relaxation
• to involve contact with others in a caring atmosphere

- to provide stimulation of the primary senses
- to increase joint range through therapeutic massage
- to minimise challenging behaviours
- to improve ability to come to attention and to maintain attention
- to increase ability to track moving objects
- to provide a stimulating environment to increase communication.

Teaching strategies
- aromatherapy
- massage
- ball pit
- tactile boards and displays
- music

- appropriate positioning
- movement through joint ranges
- water bed
- visual displays
- provide options for choice

Evaluation techniques
- video summary
- interviews with staff
- measuring joint range and movement

- observation data
- collection of quantitative data
- recording positive behaviour patterns

Key areas of curriculum framework
- Leisure and recreation

Key Competences

I: collecting, analysing, organising information

M: using mathematical ideas and techniques
C: communicating ideas and information
S: solving problems

P: planning and organising activities
T: using technology
W: working with others in teams
U: cultural understanding

Box 10.2 Mundingburra Special School MSE

Pedagogical approaches

Educators use a variety of pedagogical approaches in the mainstream classroom. These range from teacher-led through to student-led; they may involve passive learning or active learning. Four pedagogical approaches often used in the mainstream are:

- overt instruction,
- inquiry learning,
- critical framing, and
- practical learning. (Land 1997)

Overt instruction involves the teacher in presenting precise information to the students while they take notes and then use the knowledge gained to complete set exercises. The teacher is more active and the student more passive. *Inquiry learning* involves the teacher being a facilitator and student learning is through a process of assisted discovery. The student is more active and the teacher more passive. *Critical framing* requires the student to become a critic, by searching for underlying values and making judgements about the material being studied. *Practical learning* entails the student creating a product, such as a seminar or performance of some kind. Once the piece is prepared, the student shares it with the others. Here the student is active while the other students who are the audience are more passive.

A similar set of pedagogical types can be found in the MSE. Activities in the MSE can also be regarded as either being teacher-led or student-led, and students can be involved in the learning in active or passive ways. Consequently there are at least four possible pedagogical approaches:

- child-led/passive,
- child-led/active,
- teacher-led/passive,
- teacher-led/active

(see Figure 10.1).

Passive	
relaxation	positioning
attends to sense stimuli	massage
facilitative communication	self-talk/parallel-talk
watching visual display	visual stimulation
listening to music	auditory stimulation
bubble tube	FM speaker to hearing aids
sitting in beanbag, swinging chair	timing length of activity
lying on water bed	moving child to different activities
smelling aromas	providing gentle direction
plasma ball, vibrating cushion	teaching waiting skills
Child-led --------------------	-------------------- **Educator-led**
ball pit	guiding
recognising others	responding
soft play	joint range manipulation
nominating choice	repetition
start, continue, end activity	modelling
yes/no responses	prompting
requesting help, indicating need, wish	task analysis
augmentative/alternative communication	direct instruction
manipulate switches for concrete reward	backward chaining
Active	

Figure 10.1 Categorisation of pedagogical strategies for the MSE

A child-led activity could be either passive (relaxation) or active (manipulating switches for a concrete reward). Alternatively, a teacher-led activity could be passive (positioning/massage) or active (direct instruction).

It makes sense when preparing the MSE component of the child's IEP to include activities that represent all four pedagogical approaches. This helps to ensure that the child's learning environment is as comprehensive as possible and that it parallels the mainstream classroom.

Round up

Our senses enable us to learn about the world. Children use their senses to explore their environments, to learn and grow. This process of discovery continues throughout life and is the basis of our development of independence. Because of the nature of their severe, multiple learning difficulties some children miss out on valuable opportunities to explore. This problem is further compounded if the child spends most of his or her time living in a non-stimulating world. Furthermore, lack of progress coupled with lack of stimulation translates into educators and parents becoming demotivated and locked into a cycle of negativity regarding the child's future prospects.

The MSE helps to overcome these problems by providing an environment where sensory stimulation is readily available. Through the manipulation of the 37 continua (see Appendix) the MSE can be designed to match the perceived individual needs of children. The transdisciplinary team must conduct comprehensive and extensive assessment to precisely inform MSE design. This could involve assessment using the developmental approach, the adaptive behaviour approach, the environmental/ecological approach, or a combination of all three. Educators must identify suitable long-term objectives and short-term goals and use a range of pedagogical approaches to achieve these outcomes.

Figure 10.2 Drawing of a MSE by a six-year-old child.

PART IV:
Future developments

Chapter 11

Conducting research in the MSE

'*You and your students* are the only real experts about what's been occurring in your classroom and *you* can report what's been happening to other teachers. That's what we as teacher-researchers do!' . . . . Teachers want to know and to create; they are curious about their practice. Teachers hope that their research will inform that practice and lead to better teaching and learning. . . . Research can be seen . . . as the search for practical possibilities – teachers and students searching themselves, their classrooms, and their worlds for educative meaning. Such meanings are contextual and often socially constructed. Research takes on new significance for those in schools as it becomes participatory and invitational. . . . Sharing what we learn and what we know will strengthen our profession and validate what we do as informed and reflective teachers. (Burnaford *et al.* 1996, pp. xi–xii)

Introduction

A full international acceptance of the MSE as a viable educational facility is heavily dependent upon there being sufficient research evidence to support the approach. As Wang *et al.* (1990) observed, research plays an essential role in special education as the field 'seems particularly open to theories and practices, even before they are thoroughly tested'. This can be said to include the enthusiastic adoption of MSEs in educational settings despite there being a very small research base to validate their instructional relevance. Special educators therefore have a 'particular responsibility' to ensure that 'decent levels of evidence' are available before MSE practices 'enter the field in broad ways' (p. 202).

An entire chapter dedicated to conducting research has been included in this book to make the processes of research more accessible to the professionals who use the MSE. In particular it is hoped that MSE educators will be motivated to conduct their own research and to feel sufficiently confident to share their findings with others. This is the next important step if MSEs are to stay the distance.

Appropriate research

A common cry in the research literature is the need for increased levels of MSE-related research. This call, however, has tended to provide little clear direction as to what kind of research is needed, how the research could be conducted, by whom and where.

The research by occupational therapists in particular has tended to fit into the positivist paradigm because of the discipline's historical roots in the medical model. Such research broadly entails using randomised control and experimental groups, trying to keep the two groups as similar as possible except in the dimension being investigated and using 'blinded' observers, unaware of who is in which group, to make the assessment as to outcome. If there is a calculated probability of 5 per cent or less that the differences observed are due to chance, then the dimension being investigated is said to be statistically significant.

However, in MSE research, practical realities often fudge the results. Children with special needs can be extraordinarily complex and there are a large number of variables that need to be taken into consideration when assessing behaviour. It is extremely hard to make the two groups comparable in every dimension except in that of the research interest. Recognising the variables as part of the analysis requires a very large trial size to be able to generate meaningful results. Behaviour in any case is hard to quantify for comparison. Another problem is that outcome assessment is dependent on the expertise of the blinded observer and this expertise outside the MSE professionals themselves is in short supply.

Many MSE educators feel it is inappropriate to use this rigid scientific research method because it constrains and separates the teacher from that which is being researched. Importance is attached to the educational plan for each child being individualised, the teacher being responsive to the child's needs, shades and nuances being valued. There is widespread feeling that the positivist paradigm is inappropriate for the MSE. The result has been a dearth of formal MSE research, although there is a wealth of informal anecdotal experience and opinion.

MSE educators have avoided conducting their own research, putting it in the 'too-hard basket', believing that such research needs to be conducted by an academic. Paradoxically, the MSE is most research-friendly when using a constructivist paradigm. Constructivist research mostly uses qualitative research methods. Qualitative research involves systematic study to collect a depth and richness of ideographic data, looking for underlying meanings. It is acknowledged that what is observed depends on the skills and attitudes of the observer as well as attributes of the observee.

The whole MSE set-up invites the MSE educator to engage in research using qualitative methods. In order to design the MSE in ways that will stimulate each child to learn to his or her greatest potential, the educator has a responsibility to engage in ongoing high quality research. Not engaging in such research leaves the doors open for the type of criticism suggested by Mount and Cavet (1995).

> There is a danger . . . that in the absence of rigorous research the value of multisensory environments will be over estimated and, in the present situation, may be regarded as active treatment centres when, in fact, they are being used for containment, or as a dumping ground where people with learning difficulties are placed and ignored. (p. 54)

Identifying the barriers

The opening quotation maintains that the teacher is the 'only real expert' and hence is in the best position to conduct research (Burnaford *et al.* 1996, p. xi). There is an implicit assumption that such research is qualitative. The idea of the teacher researcher is an emerging concept. Borg and Gall (1989) explain

> Awareness of educational research is not sufficient to create positive attitudes toward research and the contribution it can make to the improvement of practice. There is still a long way to go before research has the respect and influence found in other professions such as medicine and engineering. Also, we have learned from research on educational change that the change process is very slow. Over the next twenty years or so, perhaps sooner, we expect to see increasing respect by practitioners for research knowledge, not as the sole guide to practice but as one basis, alongside personal judgement and experience, for making decisions. (p. 15)

Farrell (1997) identified 'insufficient interaction between research and practice in special education' as an important and common research issue. He argued that 'research does not always sufficiently emerge from practice issues. Neither are the results of research always effectively conveyed to practitioners' (p. 138–9). These separation problems between academic researcher and education practitioner and vice versa have a historical provenance. Academics now have a role to integrate theory and practice. Teachers now have a role as primary researcher.

What then are the barriers that inhibit teachers in taking on research tasks? There are several which stand out. The teacher:

1. thinks that research is conducted by researchers;
2. sees research as outside the job description of a teacher;
3. thinks there is only one type of research, namely positivist research;
4. has a fear of statistics and consequently avoids research all together;
5. believes he/she lacks the requisite skills;
6. has insufficient time to conduct research;
7. believes that research involves too much extra effort;

8 believes research too disruptive to primary teaching tasks;
9. does not have easy access to a competent research mentor;
10. has previously conducted research and been disillusioned or isolated by the process, received little support, feedback or recognition from peers or superiors;
11. is aware of, and influenced by, the MSE anti-research argument discussed in Chapter 2;
12. is afraid that findings will necessitate an unwelcome change of practice.

These twelve factors arise partly from ignorance, partly from lack of resources. This chapter aims to address lack of knowledge about research processes. Lack of resources represents short-term, usually financial, savings at the expense of long-term, more global gains. Re factor 10: good research is often its only reward.

What is research?

Research is the *systematic* investigation of an area in order to find out more about it. Teachers and therapists engage in informal research all the time. For research to become formal it must be guided by a paradigm or basic belief system.

When conducting research the researcher must choose a research paradigm which is the most appropriate to the research issue in question.

> Much of good research follows a framework developed from prior theory and research or by thought and rational deduction and this framework serves to clarify the problem and help determine the best approach to its solution. Thus the work of an excellent researcher is organized inquiry. The questions, the way they are framed, the combinations of concerns are not random. They represent approaches which help the researcher do significant research and which enable the reader to understand the point. (Anderson 1990, p. 61)

Each paradigm tends to be esoteric, carrying its own set of rules and terminology. This can make choosing an unfamiliar paradigm difficult for the novice and is the rationale for a research mentor. Furthermore, research often follows a circular pattern, through several paradigms. For example, research may begin using a constructivist paradigm, then new research may be conducted to follow up on the original findings using positivist research. This research may then be critiqued using critical theory. These three paradigms will now be described in more detail.

Research paradigms

The positivist paradigm has been a major influence in education research, especially historically in special education. Being able to make succinct statements of prediction in regard to chance life events or to planned interventions continues to be a desirable goal. But how well does the positivist paradigm achieve this?

Positivist research involves three major phases. The first is to form a theoretically-based hypothesis based on two or more constructs or variables. The second is the deduction from the hypothesis of the expected consequences in regard to these constructs. The third is to collect data to test the hypothesis. Such an approach is based on three assumptions:

- the constructs are observable,
- the world is consistent across settings and time, and
- the research is objective.

Compelling criticism has been levelled at these assumptions. In science, observable is synonymous with measurable. However in special education there is limited scope for objective measurement. (There is some, such as assessing how the number and type of MSEs vary with location or time.) Assessment of behaviour is particularly liable to observer biases intruding on the assessment. The observer inevitably interprets behaviour in the light of his or her own knowledge, skills and attitudes, that is the assessment is theory- and value-laden to a degree. Objectivity can be sought by using standardised tests, but then ultimately the construct being examined is the performance of the test rather than the behaviour itself.

In positivist research, because static universal laws are assumed to be operating, the world is therefore predictable across different settings and time. Subjects under investigation are assumed to be a representative sample of all such subjects in the world at large, and hence research observations can validly be extrapolated. Such generalisation is jeopardised by observer bias, because the possibility of different interpretation of the same behaviour obscures the construct under investigation. In special education the basis for surety that the wider population or world is indeed consistent across settings and time is a question for debate.

These criticisms had far-reaching effects and resulted in two revolutions. The first was within the positivist camp where the criticisms were acknowledged but the essential business of searching for the single objective reality, that is generalisability, remained. The second was the adoption of a second paradigm which Guba (1990a) called 'constructivism'. In this paradigm, instead of a single objective reality 'out there' for all individuals in the same category, there are assumed to be at least as many realities as there are individuals. These realities are integral and cannot be subdivided. The observed is recognised to be a function of the observer, the observee and their interaction; generalisation is therefore meaningless. Instead of comparing averages as in statistics, qualitative research yields deep, rich, idiosyncratic information. The positivist and constructivist paradigms are each based on a set of four axioms or principles. These are outlined in Table 11.1.

Table 11.1 Principal axiomatic base differences between positivist and constructivist paradigms

Axiomatic base	Positivist	Constructivist
Ontology (nature of reality)	single objective reality: dissectible into parts for testing	multiple socially constructed realities: holistic, undissectible into parts
Epistemology (relationship between known/knower.	known/knower relationship separate and objective	known/knower relationship inseparable and interactive
Purpose of research	prediction generalisation – because of laws which hold across individuals, settings, times	contextualisation generalisation unattainable, responsibility of reader to decide if transfer useful and/or appropriate
Nature of causality	suggested by statistical association	possibility of causation nonviable

The positivist researcher aims to conduct research that is value- and theory-free, whereas the constructivist researcher acknowledges that all research is value-laden and grounded in the lived experiences of the individuals being observed. These fundamental differences necessitate that each research paradigm has its own particular methods of gathering and analysing data (see Table 11.2).

Critical theory, the third paradigm listed by Guba (1990a), is 'the conceptualization of educational problems as part of the social, political, cultural, and economic patterns by which schooling is formed' (Popkewitz 1990, p. 46). Critical theory focuses on the continual contradictions that occur in schooling in this wider context. It recognises the dichotomy between 'hopes about creating a better and more equal society while, at the same time, social differentiations maintain unequal power relations and subtle forms of social regulation' (Popkewitz 1990, p. 46). For Popkewitz

> ... the practice of science in all the paradigms needs to be reconstructed with a strong sense of its social epistemology, that is, the interrelation of science with the historical conditions in which it works. Without this, science becomes procedural, technical, and one-dimensional. ... To include a disciplined sense of history into methodology and methods introduces strong questions about ethics, morality, and politics. It rejects 'seeing' the discrete events, whether bound to 'quantitative' or 'qualitative' techniques, in isolation from the relation of events to historical formations. ... History becomes a part of the analysis and logic of a science as the researched, research, and the researcher are interrelated. (p. 65)

Table 11.2 Quantitative and qualitative research methods

Method	Quantitative	Qualitative
Setting, sampling	clinical setting; random sampling; experimental and control groups	natural setting within which individual or group interacts on a regular basis; widest possible range of informants deliberately selected for observation
Instrument	testing and measuring reliable, valid, standardised norm-referenced assessment instruments	data collection using researcher as a human instrument to describe informant's perspective
Theory, data analysis	commences with hypothesis and theory which is then tested statistical analysis of numerical data	works towards inductive hypothesis and grounded theory drawn from data collected descriptive analysis of data reported in language of informant
Design	preset, with little opportunity for modification	emergent design shaped by the research process, each design unique
Outcome	little room for negotiation	outcomes tentative, involve ongoing re-examination of data for both confirming and disconfirming evidence, informant invited to take part in process

The MSE needs to be examined in the light of historical provision of services for individuals with disabilities, especially regarding the question of inclusion. Often MSEs are located within segregated special schools and are exclusively for the use of children with disabilities. Other critical theory aspects of MSE research include questions related to the social semiotics of disability (Woodill 1994) and quality of life (Bach 1994).

It is important to be aware that this chapter presents a simplified and individual interpretation of research; some people may disagree with this interpretation. As Guba (1990b) cautioned

> I recognize that what I . . . say is *my own construction*, not necessarily an objective (whatever that may be) analysis. . . . The reader should not, therefore read this chapter in the mistaken notion that it represents gospel or even a widely agreed to position. I offer it as *one* way to understand the paradigm issue. (pp. 17–18)

The purpose of this chapter is to help link research to MSEs.

Research approaches

Four research approaches that could be used in MSE research will now be briefly examined.

Ethnography

Rist (1975) described ethnography as 'the research technique of direct observation of human activity and interaction in an ongoing and naturalistic setting' (p. 86). Mertens and McLaughlin (1995) defined it as 'a research method designed to describe and analyze practices and beliefs of cultures and communities' (p. 48). In particular, ethnography is used to discover and describe the culture in educational settings. For example, ethnography could be used to study the way of life of the group of people within the MSE room – to provide a 'dynamic' picture when describing the cultural entity that is that particular MSE.

Burns (1997) argued that in ethnography the curriculum can be viewed as 'a process in which there is constant interpretation and negotiation going on among and between teachers and students, and that 'the conceptual and methodological tools of ethnography get at this aspect of curriculum planning and teaching' (p. 298). These tools of ethnography include participant observation, thick description, concern with both process and meaning, and inductive analysis.

The primary technique of ethnography is participant observation. Spradley (1980) outlined five types of participation:

1. non-participation (researcher absent, e.g. watching a videotape);
2. passive participation (researcher present but not interacting in activities);
3. moderate participation (interaction in some but not all activities);
4. active participation (interaction in all activities but not at a maximal level);
5. complete participation (full interaction in all activities).

In non-participation, being absent the researcher has more difficulty in gaining deep insight into process and meaning. In complete participation there is a problem of role conflict when trying to maintain researcher stance as well as participating in all the activities of the setting.

In the MSE the researcher could use thick description to tell the story of how the environment is being used. Thick description refers to the level of detail included in observational records. In particular the researcher aims to find out who is the group, details of the setting where the group is located, the purpose for the group coming together, the social behaviour of members of the group, the frequency and duration of activities. Data are also collected through direct observation, unstructured interviews and through document and record review.

Criteria for judging the quality of research using qualitative methods focuses on credibility, dependability, confirmability and authenticity (Guba and Lincoln

1989; Stainback and Stainback 1988). Credibility seeks to identify if there is an accurate match between the way respondents perceive social constructs and how the research represents their viewpoints. Mertens and McLaughlin (1995) listed seven strategies which can be used to enhance credibility:

1. 'prolonged and substantial engagement';
2. 'persistent observation' (observation is of sufficient length to identify pertinent features);
3. 'peer debriefing' (a disinterested peer is invited to help researcher confront own values);
4. 'negative case analysis' (ongoing re-examination of data for disconfirming evidence);
5. 'progressive subjectivity' (researcher monitors and documents own developing constructions from start of study to its end);
6. 'member checks' (researcher asks respondents to verify accuracy of data collected and interpretation);
7. 'triangulation' (checking *factual* data for consistency across different sources). (pp. 53–54)

In research using qualitative methods there is a dynamic expectation and the researcher must be responsive in the way change is recorded and reported. This process is referred to as dependability and it should be open to inspection by others through a dependability audit.

Confirmability means that the data must be able to be tracked to its source. The process of interpretation should be sufficiently explicit to be followed by others in a confirmability audit. Authenticity refers to whether the researcher is able to achieve a balanced view that takes into account all perspectives, values and beliefs.

Action research

Elliot (1991) described action research as 'the study of a social situation with a view to improving the quality of action within it' (p. 69). The purpose of action research in MSE research could be to support the transdisciplinary team, to help team members meet the challenges of practice through ongoing critical reflection. The goal of action research would be to improve the quality of teaching and therapy, learning and the learning environment. The action research process is a natural extension of everyday practice, the only difference being that the procedures are followed 'more carefully, more systematically, and more rigorously . . . and to use the relationships between these moments in the process as a source of both improvement and knowledge' (Kemmis and McTaggart 1988, p. 10).

Burns (1997) described four basic characteristics of action research.

1. Action research is *situational* – diagnosing a problem in a specific context and attempting to solve it in that context.

2. It is *collaborative*, with teams of researchers and practitioners working together.
3. It is *participatory*, as team members take part directly in implementing the research.
4. It is *self evaluative* – modifications are continuously evaluated within the ongoing situation to improve practice. (p. 347)

Action research is therefore characterised by an ongoing attempt to interlink action with reflection. For Altrichter *et al.* (1993) action research offers 'a repertoire of simple methods and strategies for researching and developing practice, which are characterised by a sensible ratio of costs to results. Methods are tailored to what is achievable without overly disrupting practice' (p. 6).

There are a number of different action research models. Lewin, the individual who first suggested the methodology, developed a seven-stage model consisting of:

1. problem identification, evaluation and formulation;
2. problem clarification by gathering the facts;
3. learning from comparable studies (formulating hypotheses);
4. considering whether the evidence is congruent with the hypothesis;
5. selection of research procedures;
6. implementation of action plan;
7. evaluation of the plan. (Burns 1997, pp. 347–52)

Altrichter *et al.* (1993) argued that 'each action research project . . . has a character of its own' (p. 6) and researchers must not allow the model to limit the research path. Their four-step model is therefore deliberately general and provides opportunity for researcher interpretation. The four steps are:

1. finding a starting point;
2. clarifying the situation;
3. developing action strategies and putting them into practice;
4. making teachers' knowledge public. (p. 7)

A third model, the action research spiral of 'plan, act and observe, reflect, revise plan, act and observe, reflect' (p. 11) was developed by Kemmis and McTaggart (1988). For Kemmis and McTaggart

> Action research establishes *self-critical communities* of people partici-
> pating and collaborating in all phases of the research process: the
> planning, the action, the observation and the reflection; it aims to build
> communities of people committed to *enlightening* themselves about the
> relationship between circumstance, action and consequence in their own
> situation, and *emancipating* themselves from the institutional and
> personal constraints which limit their power to live their own legitimate
> educational and social values. (p. 23)

Action research is well suited to MSEs because it is a systematic learning process which begins small and grows gradually. Those involved act deliberately yet are responsive to the unexpected. They seek to inform their own action through making themselves increasingly more critically aware and through practicing their own values. Through action research they may learn to theorise about their own practice and to develop a well-reasoned justification of the MSEs.

Case study

The case study involves intensive and detailed examination of a complex bounded unit. This unit may be an individual, a group or a phenomenon that is either representative or atypical. The case study can be used in both positivist and constructivist research and can involve experiment and observation. Yin (1981) defined the case study as an empirical inquiry that: '(a) Investigates a contemporary phenomenon within its real life context when (b) the boundaries between phenomenon and context are not clearly evident and in which (c) multiple sources of evidence are used' (p. 23).

In positivist research the case study is objective and is conducted in a researcher-driven setting, with an emphasis on intervention and data collection involving standardised tests. Case studies are often conducted because they help to define the parameters of the wider group of similar cases. The indepth case study thus provides potential insights into the whole group. Any attempt at generalisation, however, needs to be made with extreme caution. Multiple case studies are therefore often conducted, in order to help overcome this problem, to further define the group.

In constructivist research the case study may involve participant observation, interviewing (structured and unstructured), and document analysis. A case study may be conducted as a preliminary study in order to identify aspects that require further investigation. Borg and Gall (1989) listed five kinds of case studies that are used in education. They are:

1. 'historical case studies of organisations' (development is traced over time; for example, of a school, using interviews and documents);
2. 'observational case studies' (a focus on ongoing development of an organisation, for example, a school or classroom, over a period of time; often complex involving quantitative and qualitative research methods, especially participant observation);
3. 'oral histories' (first-person narratives obtained through extensive interviews of a single individual);
4. 'situational analysis' (a particular event is examined from each participant's viewpoint);
5. 'clinical case study' (using a variety of approaches to gain deep understanding of an individual; involves clinical observations, interviews, testing). (p. 403)

Validity is an important issue. In the positivist paradigm, the charge that the case study is 'unscientific, mainly because of its lack of research controls' (Borg and Gall 1989, p. 402) is germane and refers to *external validity*, the extent to which findings can be generalised across the group. *Internal validity,* or the extent to which changes in the independent variable are due to the intervention, can be statistically checked. Checking validity is just as important in the constructivist paradigm, although the tools, credibility, dependability, confirmability and authenticity audits, are different.

MSEs are especially suited to the case study method.

Discourse analysis

Discourse analysis is the critical examination of naturally occurring spoken, signed or written units of informal or formal conversation, through study of the organisation of language above the sentence level, to identify the contexts and cultural influences which affect its use. Two important constructs of discourse analysis are the unit of analysis, usually the entire activity setting (the people involved, their motives, goals, tasks, values, rules) and the participation structure. Participation structure provides information regarding 'the rights and obligations of participants with respect to who can say what, when, and to whom' (Cazden 1986, p. 437).

Discourse analysis may be used in socio-cultural research in education. The goal of socio-cultural research in education is to understand how 'cognitive, social, cultural, affective, and communication factors influence instruction' (Forman and McCormick 1995, p. 150). Discourse analysis permits the researcher to examine socio-cultural aspects as they occur in naturalistic settings and in real time. Discourse analysis begins with the researcher identifying 'underlying suppositions and research questions' which will be used to guide the research stages of 'design, data collection, data analysis, and interpretation' (Forman and McCormick 1995, p. 152).

To illustrate: Bozic (1997a) used discourse analysis to 'chart the ways that staff construct the purpose and meaning of multi-sensory rooms' (p. 54) in the context of special schools catering for students with multiple disabilities. Two discourse analysis approaches were used. The first was to examine 'the *linguistic resources and practices* that teachers draw upon to characterize their use of multi-sensory rooms'. This involved analysing transcripts of semi-structured interviews with staff at four UK special schools where there was a MSE to 'identify words, phrases and ways of using language that tended to be associated when teachers (and other school staff) spoke about multi-sensory rooms'. The second approach was 'to explore how the language that teachers used allowed them to *construct and describe* a viable social reality' (p. 55).

Analysis 'identified two distinct interpretative repertoires that special school staff employed when talking about their use of multi-sensory rooms: a child-led repertoire and a developmental repertoire' (p. 54). The child-led repertoire consisted of MSE descriptions which indicated that the child leads the interaction and the staff member is to provide support. The developmental repertoire consisted of MSE descriptions which indicated that the role of the staff member is to provide direction and the child is there to develop through stages. Bozic concluded that 'Analysis of transcripts demonstrated how these repertoires were deployed differently by different speakers to legitimize a range of social arrangements' (p. 54).

Getting started

Research begins by identifying the research focus, question to be answered, research problem or situation. This can be more difficult than it would initially appear because the beginning is often a time when ideas are vague and uncertain.

The next stage is to conduct a survey of the literature. This occurs in two phases. The first survey is to assist with clarifying the research problem, to help identify important terms and concepts. Once a research problem has been clearly delineated there will need to be a more extensive survey of the literature in order to guide and inform the proposed study. This second survey will provide information regarding what is currently known about the topic and what is currently not known. Information is derived to help develop a conceptual framework and to assist with interpretation of findings once the data has been collected.

The third stage of the research involves careful decision-making with regard to research paradigm, methods and design. Whichever approach is chosen, it will be necessary to consider the proposed study from an ethical perspective. Ethical issues include informed consent; confidentiality; avoidance of deception; and the need to be aware of legal constraints. If conducted in liaison with a university, often the researcher will be required to obtain ethics approval from the university ethics committee. Another issue is obtaining funding.

It is useful when conducting research to identify a critical friend that will monitor and review the research. The critical friend helps by providing an alternative perspective. This ensures that the research follows a reasonable path, that data are collected appropriately and that research reports are clear and able to be understood by others. An ideal way to learn how to conduct research and avoid pitfalls is to become actively engaged in research under the direction of someone who has had extensive experience in the research field.

The critical friend may also be able to help in preparing research reports for public presentation, either at a conference or for publication in a professional journal. Dissemination of high-quality information is the ultimate goal, to increase the knowledge base and to stimulate reflective practice. Look again at the opening quotation of this chapter.

Chapter 12

Where are we going?

Tempora mutantur, et nos mutamur in illis. (Latin, quoted in Harrison, *Description of Britain 1577*, Pt III, Ch iii): *Times change and we change with them.*

Plus ça change, plus c'est la même chose. (French, Alphonse Karr, *Les Guêpes*, 1849) *The more things change, the more they are the same.*

Introduction

No one can be certain of how the world will be in future, but study of the trends of the past and present permits some tentative prediction.

In the past 30 years there has been a shift in the range and mix of the disability spectrum as a result of medical advances. For example, retinopathy of prematurity is a relatively new disease. Genetic counselling, early diagnosis of foetal abnormality in pregnancy through ultrasound and amniocentesis, corrective foetal surgery *in utero*, elective abortion of severely abnormal foetuses, neonatal intensive care units and specialised follow-up have all had an impact. Endocrine diseases such as cretinism and metabolic diseases such as phenylketonuria are now treatable. Many physical disabilities are amenable, at least partly, to surgery. Increasing numbers of children with severe/profound multiple disabilities are surviving, for increasingly longer periods of time, living with their families and attending school.

The history of education services for children with disabilities until 40 years ago was primarily one of low expectations. Today, great strides have been made in the education of children with mild and moderate disability. Many are able to take full part in inclusion programmes (see Chapter 8). Ultimately the hope is that such children will be able to take their place in the wider society, working at their greatest potential, without prejudice with appropriate favour. However, those with severe/profound disability, especially if multiple, continue to be isolated. This population of children continues to tax the physical, emotional and economic resources of both the school community and the community overall.

Social changes

Macro-ecological considerations have implications for the MSE, with trickle-down effects to individuals and settings at the micro-ecological level. Trickle-up unfortunately is much less influential.

Currently, the more severe the learning difficulty, the more susceptible the individual is to lifelong economic hardship. Although aid in the form of technological capability and professional expertise may be available, economic rationalism usually means that those with severe/profound multiple disability continue to be at the bottom of the social pile. Of course, a mark of a civilised society is how well it takes care of its disadvantaged members. Money is not the only required commodity, social kindness and tolerance are fundamental. Inertia and lack of will are to be deprecated. 'Patchy' best describes the present situation in Western society.

From public resentment of professionals maintaining a monopolistic authority over information has come an anti-professionalism backlash. The fallout has been that professionals are changing the way they deal with the public, being more open and accountable in their processes. This has been of benefit to all, for professionals are part of the wider public too. However there is also a populist push for a 'quick fix' even for complex issues, and a 'blame mentality' if a situation fails to be amenable to such an approach. It is inevitable the pendulum will swing back again to valuing professional input, especially under the barrage of unsorted information now increasingly easily available through technology. This time though, professional input will need to be more inclusive, more focused on acknowledging the essential dignity of the individual, regardless of ability or disposition.

Technological changes

The most striking facet of change in the last 30 years is the technological revolution, simplifying many time-consuming tasks and enabling new tasks, previously unthought of, to be performed. This technology covers a wide gamut from electronics through to computers. Technology is at the forefront of the child's education at both a macro and a micro level, enabling educators to expand their repertoire of teaching practices and enabling the student to have enhanced opportunities for developing skills in relation to communication, daily living and socialisation.

The dependence on information and communication technology for all sections of the community means that it can only increase. The computer, the telephone, the facsimile machine, the television, the radio, the video – all are powerful tools if used appropriately. Used inappropriately, they can frustrate, waste time and money, dehumanise interactions and generally be counter-productive. Technology has the potential to create a burgeoning sea of information through which the transdisciplinary team has to navigate.

A generation in computer terms, is now only eighteen months. To facilitate appropriate use of computers there is therefore a need for generic computing skills, rather than for specific packages. There is currently a wide variation in the degree of computer literacy among educators. It is conceivable that, in future, failure to use information technology could be regarded as professional negligence. This is a distressing concept for the majority of educators who have had no formal training in information technology and for whom such illiteracy will become increasingly burdensome. Even more distressing for those who deliberately chose to work in special education thinking they would somehow be shielded from impending changes taking place in the wider community.

The new technology is redefining the learning environment itself, helping to make those with a disability more independent and more able to access and even help shape the mainstream. Examples include optical scanners that have Braille, audio or large-print format (meaning children with visual impairment can participate in classrooms where the class teacher does not know Braille), electric wheelchairs, increasing the mobility of those with severe physical disabilities (meaning a carer is no longer necessary to ensure physical or functional inclusion), voice output communication systems for individuals with severe communication disorders (meaning those who cannot speak at last have a voice), teletypewriter telephones and teletext decoders for the Deaf (meaning those who cannot hear are able to link up with each other and the hearing world).

Inclusion now enables children with disabilities to have access to computer keyboard technology as do their non-disabled peers. Furthermore, other technology is available to ensure that the child with a learning difficulty is able to access a curriculum which matches his or her individual needs and learning style. The new technologies are helping to reconstruct a much more diverse interpretation of what 'the mainstream' means. A mainstream that cannot boast diversity in both breadth and depth will seem shallow and inconsequential. In the future it is likely that individuals with disabilities will have much more profound influences on the essential nature of what the mainstream means. This may take us into areas which have as yet remained largely unexplored.

Computer technology is currently used by educators for assessment, record-keeping, report generation, providing links to databases, libraries and discussion groups. E-mails and facsimilies are used to communicate with other members of the transdisciplinary team and to consult with outside experts. Computers can also be used to design the MSE so that the space can be much more multifunctional in nature. Input can be obtained from all transdisciplinary team members, members of the population who are disabled, specialists in industrial psychology, architecture and design the world over. Furthermore, the design can continually develop.

World Wide Web

The interface of computing and communications is regarded as the defining characteristic of the information age. Digitalisation of information and global communications have resulted in the Internet and in its populist form, the World Wide Web (WWW). One of the principal effects of the WWW has been to allow individuals easily to become publishers of information with a world-wide audience. This democratisation of information will change the nature of those institutions for which arcane knowledge is the passport for entry.

For educators, the WWW has facilitated access to information, for example, about a particular disability type or educational approach. All the major journals are now on the WWW; there is even a view that the paper journal is a dinosaur near extinction. The WWW facilitates discussion groups brainstorming subjects of mutual interest often across national barriers, such as the MSE. As parents also turn to WWW sites for information and become more educationally literate, the demand for negotiation and collaboration will continue to increase.

The number of websites is increasing exponentially. As yet there is no agreed protocol for the evaluation and updating of websites, although there is a WWW consortium which sets international standards and which has a number of working parties examining these issues. A major caveat is that an ability to surf the Net is not synonymous with being skilled in the collation, distillation and application of the information. Understanding how to use information technology is only one component of this broader discipline.

Virtual reality

Virtual reality (VR) is a computer generated interactive display which gives a very strong impression of three dimensionality and, being responsive to the user's movements, of being real. Largely used for entertainment at present, this technology has enormous potential in disability education once the costs have been contained. VR will give students access to simulations of otherwise inaccessible experiences.

A high degree of immersion can be generated by a head-mounted display, which blocks out vision of the real world to present a wide angle virtual scene. The computer tracks movement of the head, so as the user looks in different directions, the view of the virtual scene changes, very much as the view of a real scene would. The user operates controls and thereby alters elements within the virtual scene. It is to be anticipated that in regard to children with special needs, future developments will:

- reduce the weight of the helmet,
- modify the types of controls available,
- use electromyogram signals in relation to eye and muscle movement to activate the controls for those with very little physical movement,
- link the educator into the student's virtual scene,
- intermesh, even more precisely than at present, user action with scenic viewpoint both spatially and temporally, and
- in general make VR more user-friendly.

The same virtual scene can be explored in different ways by different students or by the same student at different times. VR is a highly-interactive, flexible tool and therefore strongly encourages active learning. VR would seem to have 'very significant potential for addressing individual educational needs, and enlarging the range of educational experiences available to students' (Ainge 1995, p. 27). As such, it would seem that it will be an important addition to the MSE armamentarium; the MSE could be a totally virtual space. However the physical and mental consequences of spending long times immersed in virtual environments are simply not known. The ramifications of VR for children with disabilities are yet to be explored in any depth.

MSE

I see the MSE of particular use for those with severe/profound multiple disability, although it has relevance for other disability subgroups and even for the mainstream. The group with severe/profound multiple disability is the group that conventional education approaches have been least able to help. The MSE can be a key to open the door to development of these students' highest potential and to date educationalists have not found many such keys.

I can remember when I was teaching in a regular primary school there was a child who was being treated for cancer. On the days when he received chemotherapy he would still want to come to school, so we created a special environment for him that he could access if he felt sick or needed his own space. It was a little room made out of a tent with a beanbag, a cassette recorder with headphones, some corn chips to nibble on and his own special things to make him feel better. In retrospect, this tent could be viewed as a MSE, giving him control over when he was a part of the regular classroom and when he was not. His parents constantly told us that this greatly changed the quality of his life.

During a recent visit to an early childhood centre, a class teacher told me about a child with a behaviour problem that she was having difficulty including in the regular programme. The learning environment needed to be rearranged to suit the observed needs of this particular child. The more regular schools include children with learning difficulties, the more the classroom of the future is likely to be a multifaceted environment. It may just contain a MSE to provide time out for the child who is finding it too difficult to cope in the mainstream class.

The MSE is constantly being defined and redefined. Currently the concept of the MSE as a fixed location is being challenged, for example portable MSEs are being constructed consisting of fold out boxes or quilts which can be stored when not in use (Bishop 1998). They can be easily transported to children in isolated and rural areas. Another advantage is that the child is not locked into one environment. He or she can move on to a more complicated portable MSE when the time is right.

Undoubtedly in years to come new aspects of the MSE will emerge. There is an exciting future for the MSE ahead, through thoughtful research and development which I hope, to some extent, has been fostered by this book.

Appendix

MSE continua

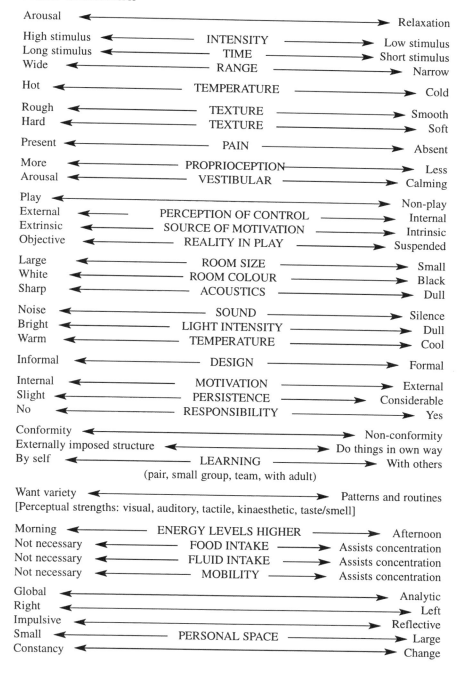

Arousal ←——————————————————————————→ Relaxation

High stimulus ←——— INTENSITY ———→ Low stimulus
Long stimulus ←——— TIME ———→ Short stimulus
Wide ←——— RANGE ———→ Narrow

Hot ←——— TEMPERATURE ———→ Cold

Rough ←——— TEXTURE ———→ Smooth
Hard ←——— TEXTURE ———→ Soft

Present ←——— PAIN ———→ Absent

More ←——— PROPRIOCEPTION ———→ Less
Arousal ←——— VESTIBULAR ———→ Calming

Play ←——————————————————————————→ Non-play
External ←——— PERCEPTION OF CONTROL ———→ Internal
Extrinsic ←——— SOURCE OF MOTIVATION ———→ Intrinsic
Objective ←——— REALITY IN PLAY ———→ Suspended

Large ←——— ROOM SIZE ———→ Small
White ←——— ROOM COLOUR ———→ Black
Sharp ←——— ACOUSTICS ———→ Dull

Noise ←——— SOUND ———→ Silence
Bright ←——— LIGHT INTENSITY ———→ Dull
Warm ←——— TEMPERATURE ———→ Cool

Informal ←——— DESIGN ———→ Formal

Internal ←——— MOTIVATION ———→ External
Slight ←——— PERSISTENCE ———→ Considerable
No ←——— RESPONSIBILITY ———→ Yes

Conformity ←——————————————————————————→ Non-conformity
Externally imposed structure ←——————→ Do things in own way
By self ←——— LEARNING ———→ With others
(pair, small group, team, with adult)

Want variety ←——————————————————————————→ Patterns and routines
[Perceptual strengths: visual, auditory, tactile, kinaesthetic, taste/smell]

Morning ←——— ENERGY LEVELS HIGHER ———→ Afternoon
Not necessary ←——— FOOD INTAKE ———→ Assists concentration
Not necessary ←——— FLUID INTAKE ———→ Assists concentration
Not necessary ←——— MOBILITY ———→ Assists concentration

Global ←——————————————————————————→ Analytic
Right ←——————————————————————————→ Left
Impulsive ←——————————————————————————→ Reflective
Small ←——— PERSONAL SPACE ———→ Large
Constancy ←——————————————————————————→ Change

References

Addis, C. (not dated) *Using Switches and Switching Systems with People who have Severe Learning Difficulties.* Chesterfield, Derbyshire: Rompa.

Ainge, D. (1995) 'Virtual reality in Townsville schools', *Special Education Matters* **6**, 25–27.

Aitken, S. and Buultjens, M. (1992) *Vision For Doing: Assessing Functional Vision of Learners who are Multiply Disabled.* Edinburgh: Moray House Publications.

Alchin, A. M. and Pagliano, P. J. (1988) 'The parent checklist: how effective is it in isolating children with vision problems?' in *Toy Libraries and Special Education Working Together: Proceedings of the AASE (Qld) Conference.* Cairns: Australian Association of Special Education.

Alrichter, H., Posch, P., Somekh, B. (1993) *Teachers Investigate their Work: An Introduction to the Methods of Action Research.* London: Routledge.

American Association on Mental Retardation (1992) *Mental Retardation, Classification, and System of Support* , 9th edn. Washington, DC: AAMR.

Anderson, G. (1990) *Fundamentals of Educational Research.* London: Falmer Press.

Ashby, M. *et al.* (1995) 'Snoezelen: its effects on concentration and responsiveness in people with profound multiple handicaps', *British Journal of Occupational Therapy* **58**(7), 303–7.

Ashman, A. and Elkins, J. (1997) 'Learning opportunities for all children', in Ashman, A. and Elkins, J. (eds) *Educating Children with Special Needs,* 5–38, 3rd edn. Sydney, Australia: Prentice-Hall.

Ayres, A. J. (1979) *Sensory Integration and the Child.* Los Angeles, CA: Western Psychological Services.

Ayres, A. J. (1989) *Sensory Integration and Praxis Tests.* Los Angeles, CA: Western Psychological Services.

Ayres, M. (1994) 'Designing for sensory experience', *Eye Contact* **10**, 29–30.

Bach, M. (1994) 'Quality of life: questioning the vantage points for research', in Rioux, M. H. and Bach M. (eds) *Disability is Not Measles: New Research Paradigms in Disability,* 127–151. New York, Ontario: L'Institut Roeher Institute.

Bagnato, S. J. and Neisworth, J. T. (1991) *Assessment for Early Intervention: Best Practices for Professionals.* New York, NY: Guilford Press.

Bailey, D. B. and Wolery, M. (1984) *Teaching Infants and Preschoolers with Handicaps.* Columbus, OH: Merrill.

Baker, R. *et al.* (1997) 'Snoezelen: its long-term and short-term effects on older people with dementia', *British Journal of Occupational Therapy* **60**(5), 213–8.

Bank-Mikkelsen, N. (1969) 'A metropolitan area in Denmark: Copenhagen', in Kugel, R. and Wolfenberger, W. (eds) *Issues in Special Education,* 42–50. Mountain View, CA: Mayfield Publishing.

Barraga, N. (1964) *Increased Visual Behavior in Low Vision Children.* New York, NY: American Foundation for the Blind.

Barraga, N. (1974) 'Perceptual development in low vision children: a practical approach'. *Proceedings of the Australian and New Zealand Association of Teachers of the Visually Handicapped Conference,* 1–10. Brisbane, Australia: ANZAEVH.

Barraga, N. (1983) *Visual Handicap and Learning,* rev. edn. Austin, TX: Exceptional Resources.

Berger, E. H. (1991) *Parents as Partners in Education: The School and Home Working Together,* 3rd edn. New York, NY: Merrill.

Best, A. B. (1992) *Teaching Children with Visual Impairments.* Milton Keynes: Open University Press.

Bigge, J. L. (ed.) (1991) *Teaching Individuals with Physical and Multiple Disabilities,* 3rd edn. New York, NY: Merrill.

Bishop, K. (1998) *Play equipment for children with disabilities*, paper presented at the Third Biennial National Early Intervention Conference, AJC Convention and Exhibition Centre, Sydney, Australia.

Bloemhard, L. (1992) 'Snoezelen met demente bejaarden maakt weken voor verzorgenden aangenamer', *Verpleegkunde Nieuws Nr* **21**, 21–5.

Bondurant-Utz, J. A. (1994) 'Ecological and behavioral assessments' in Bondurant-Utz, J. A. and Luciano, L. B. (eds) *A Practical Guide to Infant and Preschool Assessment in Special Education,* 181–98. Needham Heights, MA: Allyn and Bacon.

Borg, W. and Gall, M. (1989) *Educational Research: An Introduction,* 5th edn. New York, NY: Longman.

Bowd, A. (1990) *Exceptional Children in Class.* North Melbourne, Australia: Hargreen.

Bower, E. M. (1989) *Early Identification of Emotionally Handicapped Children in School,* 3rd edn. Springfield, IL: Charles C. Thomas.

Bower, H. (1967) 'Sensory stimulation and the treatment of senile demensia', *The Medical Journal of Australia* **22,** 1113–19.

Bozic, N. (1997a) 'Constructing the room: multisensory rooms in educational contexts', *European Journal of Special Needs Education* **12**(1), 54–70.

Bozic, N. (1997b) 'Educational technology', in Mason H. and McCall S. (eds) *Visual Impairment: Access to Education for Children and Young People,* 335–44. London: David Fulton Publishers.

Bozic, N. and Murdoch, H. (1994) *Distance Education Course for Multi-Sensory Impairment (SEEP 30: Unit 4 Specialized Environments).* Birmingham: Faculty of Education and Continuing Studies, University of Birmingham.

Brown, F. and Snell, M. (1993) 'Meaningful assessment', in Snell, M. E. (ed.) *Instruction of Students with Severe Disabilities,* 61–98, 4th edn. New York, NY: Merrill.

Brown, F., *et al.* (1979) 'A strategy for developing chronological-age-appropriate and functional curricular content for severely handicapped adolescents and young adults', *Journal of Special Education* **13,** 81–90.

Bundy, A. C. (1991) 'Play theory and sensory integration' in Fisher, A. G., Murray, E. A., Bundy, A. C. (eds) *Sensory Integration: Theory and Practice,* 46–68. Philadelphia: F. A. Davis.

Burnaford, G., Fischer, J., Hobson, D. (1996) 'Preface', in Burnaford, G., Fischer, J., Hobson, D. (eds) *Teachers Doing Research: Practical Possibilities,* xi–xii. Mahwah, NJ: Lawrence Erlbaum Associates,.

Burns, R. B. (1997) *Introduction to Research Methods,* 3rd edn, South Melbourne, Australia: Addison Wesley Longman.

Buultjens, M. (1997) 'Functional Vision Assessment and Development in Children' in Mason, H. and McCall S. (eds) *Visual Impairment: Access to Education for Children and Young People,* 345–54. London: David Fulton Publishers.

Byers, R. and Rose, R. (1996) 'Schools Should Decide ...' in Rose, R. *et al.* (eds) *Implementing the Whole Curriculum for Pupils with Learning Difficulties,* 1–13. London: David Fulton Publishers.

Campbell, P. H. (1993) 'Physical management and handling procedures', in Snell, M. E. (ed.) *Instruction of Students with Severe Disabilities,* 248–63, 4th edn. New York, NY: Merrill.

Cavet, J. and Mount, H. (1995) 'Multisensory environments', in Hogg, J. and Cavet, J. (eds) *Making Leisure Provision for People with Profound Learning and Multiple Disabilities,* 67–85. London: Chapman Hall.

Cazden, C. B. (1986) 'Classroom Discourse', in Wittrock, M. C. (ed.) *Handbook of Research on Teaching,* 3rd edn, 432–463. New York, NY: Macmillan.

Cleland, C. C. and Clark, C. M. (1966) 'Sensory deprivation and aberrant behavior among idiots', *American Journal of Mental Deficiency* **71,** 213–25.

Connell, R. (1990) 'Curriculum and social justice: why is education and social justice an issue?' *Queensland Teachers Union Professional Magazine* **8**(3), 7–11.

Crossley, R. (1992) 'Getting the words out: case studies in facilitated communication training', *Topics in Language Disorders* **12**(4), 46–59.

Crowther, F. (1998) Leading schools – planning the future. A research-based framework for enhancing school outcomes: a proposal for site based managers, *Education Views* **7**(8), i–iv.

Cummins, R. A. (1992) *Comprehensive Quality of Life Scale – Intellectual Disability, ComQol-ID Manual,* 3rd. edn. Melbourne, Australia: Deakin University.

Cunningham, C. C., Hutchinson, R., Kewin, J. (1991) 'Recreation for people with profound and severe learning difficulties: The Wittington Hall Snoezelen project', in Hutchinson, R. (ed.) *The Whittington Hall Snoezelen Project: A Report from Inception to the End of the First Twelve Months.* Chesterfield: North Derbyshire Health Authority.

Dale, F. J. (1990) *The Stimulation Guide.* Cambridge: Woolhead-Faulkner.

de Bunsen, A. (1994) 'A study in the use and implications of the Snoezelen resource at Limington House School', in Hutchinson, R. and Kewin, J. (eds) *Sensations and Disability: Sensory Environments for Leisure, Snoezelen, Education and Therapy,* 138–62. Chesterfield, Derbyshire: Rompa.

Department for Education (1994) *Code of Practice on the Identification and Assessment of Special Educational Needs*. London: DfE.

Diffey, B. (1993) 'Ultraviolet black lamps for visual stimulation: is there a risk to health?' *Information Exchange,* December, 10–1.

Dunn, R. S. and Dunn, K. (1992) *Teaching Elementary Students Through Their Individual Learning Styles: Practical Approaches for Grade 3–6.* Needham Heights, MA: Allyn and Bacon.

Dunnett, J. (1997) 'Nielsen's little room: its use with a young blind and physically disabled child', *Journal of Visual Impairment and Blindness* **91**, 145–50.

Dyson, A. (1997) 'Social and educational disadvantage: reconnecting special needs education', *British Journal of Special Education* **24**, 152–7.

Edwards, B. (1992) 'Tactile boards', *Information Exchange,* November, 12–13.

Elkins, J. (1997) 'The school context', in Ashman, A. and Elkins, J. (eds) *Educating Children with Special Needs*, 67–101, 3rd edn. Sydney, Australia: Prentice-Hall.

Elliot, J. (1991). *Action Research for Educational Change.* Milton Keynes: Open University.

Evans, I. M. and Scotti, J. R. (1989) 'Defining meaningful outcomes for persons with profound disabilities', in Brown, F. and Lehr, D. (eds) *Persons with Profound Disabilities: Issues and Practices*, 83–108. Baltimore, MD: Paul H. Brookes Publishing.

Farrell, M. (1997) *The Special Education Handbook.* London: David Fulton Publishers.

Finnie, N. R. (1975) *Handling the Young Cerebral Palsied Child at Home.* New York, NY: E. P. Dutton.

Fisher, A. G. and Murray, E. A. (1991) 'Introduction to sensory integration theory', in Fisher, A. G., Murray, E. A., Bundy, A. C. (eds) *Sensory Integration: Theory and Practice*, 3–26. Philadelphia: F. A. Davis.

Forman, E. A. and McCormick, D. (1995) 'Discourse analysis: a sociocultural perspective', *Remedial and Special Education* **16**, 150–58.

Fraiberg, S. (1977) *Insights from the Blind: Comparative Studies of Blind and Sighted Infants.* New York, NY: Basic Books.

Frankenberger, W. and Harper, J. (1988) 'States' definitions and procedures for identifying children with mental retardation: comparison of 1981–1982 and 1985–1986 guidelines, *Mental Retardation* **26**, 133–36.

Friend, M. P. and Cook, L. (1992) *Interactions: Collaboration Skills for School Professionals.* New York, NY: Longman.

Fulcher, G. (1989) *Disabling Policies? A Comparative Approach to Education Policy and Disability.* London: Falmer Press.

Gallagher, M. and Balson, M. (1994) 'Snoezelen in education', in Hutchinson, R. and Kewin, J. (eds) *Sensations and Disability: Sensory Environments for Leisure, Snoezelen, Education and Therapy*, 129–37. Chesterfield, Derbyshire: Rompa.

Gaylord-Ross, R. J. and Holvoet, J. F. (1985) *Strategies for Educating Students with Severe Handicaps.* Boston, MA: Little, Brown.

Gilbert, R. and Low, P. (1994) 'Discourse and power in education: analysing institutional processes in schools', *Australian Educational Researcher* **21**(3), 1–24.

Giorcelli, L. (1993) 'Creating a counter-hegemonic school: a model for the education of children with disabilities', *Social Justice, Equity and Dilemmas of Disability in Education,* 85–95. Queensland, Australia: Department of Education.

Glenn, S., Cunningham, C., Shorrock, A. (1996) 'Social interaction in multisensory environments', in Bozic, N. and Murdoch, H. (eds) *Learning Through Interaction: Technology and Children with Multiple Disabilities,* 66–82. London: David Fulton Publishers.

Goode, D. (1990) 'Thinking about and discussing quality of life', in Schalock, R. and Begab, M. (eds) *Quality Of Life: Perspectives and Issues.* Washington, DC: American Association on Mental Retardation.

Goossens, C., Crain, S. S., Elder, P. S. (1994) *Engineering the Preschool Environment for Interactive Symbolic Communication.* Birmingham, AL: Southeast Augmentative Communication Conference Publications.

Gray, M. (1994) 'Multi-sensory rooms – the views continue', *Eye Contact* **8**, 17–18.

Griffin, P. (1998) 'Outcomes and profiles: changes in teachers' assessment practices', *Curriculum Perspectives* **18**, 9–19.

Grossman, H. J. (ed.) (1983) *Classification in Mental Retardation.* Washington, DC: American Association on Mental Deficiency.

Guba, E. G. (1990a) 'Foreword', in Guba, E. G. (ed.) *The Paradigm Dialogue*, 9–14. Newbury Park, CA: Sage Publications.

Guba, E. G. (1990b) 'The alternative paradigm dialogue', in Guba, E. G. (ed.) *The Paradigm Dialogue,* 17–30. Newbury Park, CA: Sage Publications.

Guba, E. G. and Lincoln, Y. S. (1989) *Fourth Generation Evaluation.* Newbury Park, CA: Sage Publications.

Haggar, L. and Hutchison, R. (1991) 'Snoezelen: an approach to the provision of a leisure resource for people with profound and multiple handicaps', *Mental Handicap* **19**, 51–5.

Halpern, A. S. (1989) 'A systematic approach to transition programming for adolescents and young adults with disabilities', *Australia and New Zealand Journal of Developmental Disabilities* **15**, 1–13.

Halpern, A. S. (1994) 'Quality of life for students with disabilities in transition from school to adulthood', *Social Indicators Research* **33**, 193–236.

Hatton, E. and Elliot, R. (1994) 'Social justice and the provision of education', in Hatton, E. (ed.) *Understanding Teaching: Curriculum and the Social Context of Schooling,* 71–83. Sydney: Harcourt Brace.

Henning, D. (1994) 'Snoezelen and self injury', in Hutchinson, R. and Kewin, J. (eds) *Sensations and Disability: Sensory Environments for Leisure, Snoezelen, Education and Therapy,* 109–19. Chesterfield, Derbyshire: Rompa.

Hepworth, M. (1993) *The Use of the Multi-Sensory Room with Multi-Sensory Impaired Children.* B.Phil.Ed. dissertation, University of Birmingham, UK.

Hill, E. W. and Hill, M. M. (1980) 'Revision and validation of a test for assessing conceptual abilities of visually impaired children', *Journal of Visual Impairment and Blindness* **74**, 373–80.

Hirstwood, R. and Gray, M. (1995) *A Practical Guide to the Use of Multi-Sensory Rooms.* Leicestershire, UK: Toys for the Handicapped.

Hirstwood, R. and Smith, C. (1996) 'Developing competencies in multi-sensory rooms', in Bozic, N. and Murdoch, H. (eds) *Learning Through Interaction: Technology and Children with Multiple Disabilities,* 83–91. London: David Fulton Publishers.

Hopkins, P. and Willetts, D. (1993) 'And also . . .', *Eye Contact* **6**, 26.

Hopkins, P., Willetts, D., Orr, R. (1994) *Multisensory Environments: A Code of Practice.* London: RNIB (unpublished).

Hulsegge, J. and Verheul, A. (1986 original Dutch edition; 1987 English translation by R. Alink) *Snoezelen Another World: A Practical Book of Sensory Experience Environments for the Mentally Handicapped.* Chesterfield, UK: Rompa.

Hutchinson, R. (ed.) (1991) *The Whittington Hall Snoezelen Project: A Report From Inception to the End of the First Twelve Months.* Chesterfield: North Derbyshire Health Authority.

Hutchinson, R. and Haggar, L. (1991) 'The development and evaluation of a Snoezelen leisure resource for people with profound and multiple handicaps', in Hutchinson, R. (ed.) *The Whittington Hall Snoezelen Project: A Report From Inception to the End of the First Twelve Months.* Chesterfield: North Derbyshire Health Authority.

Hutchinson, R. and Haggar, L. (1994) 'The development and evaluation of a Snoezelen leisure resource for people with severe multiple disability', in Hutchinson, R. and Kewin, J. (eds) *Sensations and Disability: Sensory Environments for Leisure, Snoezelen, Education and Therapy,* 18–48. Chesterfield, Derbyshire: Rompa.

Kaiser, A. P. (1993) 'Functional language', in Snell, M. E. (ed.) *Instruction of Students with Severe Disabilities,* 347–379, 4th edn. New York, NY: Merrill.

Kauffman, J. M. (ed.) (1989) *Characteristics of Behavior Disorders of Children and Youth,* 4th edn. Columbus, OH: Merrill.

Kemmis, S. and McTaggart, R. (1988) *The Action Research Planner,* 3rd edn. Victoria, Australia: Deakin University.

Kewin, J. (1991a) 'Snoezelen user guide', in Hutchinson, R. (ed.) *The Whittington Hall Snoezelen Project: A Report From Inception to the End of the First Twelve Months.* Chesterfield: North Derbyshire Health Authority.

Kewin, J. (1991b) 'Snoezelen – pulling the strands together', in Hutchinson, R. (ed.) *The Whittington Hall Snoezelen Project: A Report From Inception to the End of the First Twelve Months.* Chesterfield: North Derbyshire Health Authority.

Kewin, J. (1991c) 'Snoezelen: essentials and basics (some thoughts about design)', in Hutchinson, R. (ed.) *The Whittington Hall Snoezelen Project: A Report From Inception to the End of the First Twelve Months.* Chesterfield: North Derbyshire Health Authority.

Kewin, J. (1994a) 'Snoezelen – the reasons and the method', in Hutchinson, R. and Kewin, J. (eds) *Sensations and Disability: Sensory Environments for Leisure, Snoezelen, Education and Therapy,* 6–17. Chesterfield, Derbyshire: Rompa.

Kewin, J. (1994b) 'Snoezelen environments – a management perspective', in Hutchinson, R. and Kewin J. (eds) *Sensations and Disability: Sensory Environments for Leisure, Snoezelen, Education and Therapy*, 120–8. Chesterfield, Derbyshire: Rompa.

Kirk, S. A. and Gallagher, J. J. (1989) *Educating Exceptional Children*, 3rd edn. Boston, MA: Houghton Mifflin.

Kneedler, R. D., Hallihan, D. P., Kauffman, J. M. (1984) *Special Education for Today*. Englewood Cliffs, NJ: Prentice-Hall.

Lacey, P. and Lomas, J. (1993) *Support Services and the Curriculum: A Practical Guide to Collaboration*. London: David Fulton Publishers.

LaGrow, S. J. *et al.* (1998) 'The effects on visually impaired children of viewing fluorescent stimuli under black-light conditions', *Journal of Visual Impairment and Blindness* **92**, 313–21.

Land, R. (1997) 'Pedagogies of the political', in Land, R. (ed.) *Education for Responsible Citizenship: Classroom Units for Primary and Secondary Teachers*, 1–18. Adelaide: Social Education Association of Australia.

Laurent, S. (1992) 'Atmospherics', *Information Exchange,* November, 19.

Lewis, R. and Doorlag, D. (1987) *Teaching Special Students in the Mainstream*. Columbus, OH: Merrill.

Liederman, P. H. *et al.* (1958) 'Sensory deprivation: clinical aspects', *Archives Internal Medicine* **101**, 389.

Light, J. (1989) 'Towards a definition of communicative competence for individuals using Augmentative and Alternative Communication Systems', *Augmentative and Alternative Communication* **5**, 137–44.

Light, J. and McNaughton, D. (1993) 'Literacy and Augmentative and Alternative Communication (AAC): the expectations and priorities of parents and teachers', *Topics in Language Disorders* **13**(2) 33–46.

Lister, S. A. (1993) *A Study of the Use of Dark Multi-Sensory Environments, with Multi-Sensory Impaired Children Within a LEA's Special School*. B.Phil.Ed. (MSI) dissertation, University of Birmingham, UK.

Long, A. P. and Haig, L. (1992) 'How do clients benefit from Snoezelen? An exploratory study', *British Journal of Occupational Therapy* **55**(3), 103–6.

Longhorn, F. (1988) *A Sensory Curriculum for Very Special People*. London: Souvenir Press.

Luciano, L. B. (1994) 'Qualitative observations of assessment behavior' in Bondurant-Utz, J. A. and Luciano, L. B. (eds) *A Practical Guide to Infant and Preschool Assessment in Special Education,* 27–40. Needham Heights, MA: Allyn and Bacon.

Luetke-Stahlman, B. and Luckner, J. (1991) *Effectively Educating Students with Hearing Impairments*. New York, NY: Longman.

McKee, *et al.* (1983) *Occupational and Physical Therapy Services in School-Based Programs: Organizational Manual*. Houston, TX: Psychological Services Division, Harris County Department of Education.

McLarty, M. (1993) 'Soap opera or bubble tube?' *Eye Contact* **7**, 11–12.

Manor, M. (1994) 'Learning curves', *Information Exchange,* July, 23–32.

Mason, H. (1997) 'Assessment of vision' in Mason, H. and McCall, S. (eds) *Visual Impairment: Access to Education for Children and Young People,* 51–63. London: David Fulton Publishers.

Melberg, M. and Jansson, G. (1994) 'Balders Hus (the house of Balder), The old house with the new ideas', In Hutchinson, R. and Kewin, J. (eds) *Sensations and Disability: Sensory Environments for Leisure, Snoezelen, Education and Therapy,* 163–71. Chesterfield, Derbyshire: Rompa.

Mertens, D. M., and McLaughlin, J. A. (1995) *Research Methods in Special Education*. London: Sage Publications.

Mirenda, P. and Calculator, S. (1993) 'Enhancing curricular designs', in Kupper, L. (ed.) *The National Symposium on Effective Communication for Children and Youth with Severe Disabilities: Topic Papers, Reader's Guide and Video Tape*, 253–280.

Mithaug, D. (1991) *Self-Determined Kids: Raising Satisfied and Successful Children*. New York: Macmillan (Lexington imprint).

Mithaug, D. *et al.* (1988) *Why Special Education Graduates Fail: How to Teach Them to Succeed*. Colorado Springs, CO: Ascent Publications.

Moffat, N. *et al.* (1993) *Snoezelen®: An Experience for People with Dementia*. Chesterfield, Derbyshire: Rompa.

Moore, A., Harris, G., Stephens, J. (1994) 'People with a disability – therapists and sensory activity', in Hutchinson, R. and Kewin, J. (eds) *Sensations and Disability: Sensory Environments for Leisure, Snoezelen, Education and Therapy*, 88–108. Chesterfield, Derbyshire: Rompa.

Moore, W. (1991) 'Snoezelen' (letter), *Mental Handicap* **19**, 126.

Morse, M. T. (1990) 'Cortical visual impairment in young children with multiple disabilities', *Journal of Visual Impairment and Blindness* **84**, 200–203.

Mount, H. (1993) 'Window box: creating a multi-sensory garden', *Information Exchange,* July, 24–5.

Mount, H. and Cavet, J. (1995) 'Multisensory environments: an exploration of their potential for young people with profound and multiple learning difficulties', *British Journal of Special Education* **22**, 52–5.

National Council for Educational Technology (1993) *An Introduction to the Use of the Multisensory Environment.* Coventry: Special Needs Resources.

Neisworth, J. T. and Bagnato, S. J. (1988) 'Assessment in early childhood special education: a typology of dependent measures', in Odom, S. L. and Karnes, M. B. (eds) *Early Intervention for Infants and Children with Handicaps: An Empirical Base,* 23–51. Baltimore, MD: Paul H. Brookes Publishing.

Nielsen, L. (1979) *The Comprehending Hand.* Copenhagen, Denmark: Socialstyrelsen.

Nielsen, L. (1988) *Spatial Relations in Congenitally Blind Infants.* Kalundborg, Denmark: Refsnaesskolen.

Nielsen, L. (1990a) *The Visually Impaired Child's Early Abilities, Behaviour, Learning.* Copenhagen, Denmark: SIKON.

Nielsen, L. (1990b) *Are You Blind?* Copenhagen, Denmark: SIKON.

Nielsen, L. (1991) 'Spatial relations in congenitally blind infants: a study', *Journal of Visual Impairment and Blindness* **85**, 11–16.

Nielsen, L. (1992a) *Educational Approaches.* Copenhagen, Denmark: SIKON.

Nielsen, L. (1992b) *Space and Self.* Copenhagen, Denmark: SIKON.

Nielsen, L. (1993a) 'The blind child's ability to listen', *Information Exchange,* March, 12–14.

Nielsen, L. (1993b) *Early Learning, Step by Step in Children with Vision Impairment and Multiple Disabilities.* Copenhagen, Denmark: SIKON.

Nielsen, L. (1994a) 'Learning object concept and permanence in blind infants', *Information Exchange,* March, 19–23.

Nielsen, L. (1994b) 'The Essef board: facilitating the child's learning to stand and walk', *Information Exchange,* December, 22–23.

Nihira, K. *et al.* (1974) *Manual of the AAMD Adaptive Behavior Scale.* Washington, DC: American Association on Mental Deficiency.

O'Brien, J. (1987) 'A guide to personal futures planning planning', in Bellamy, G. T. and Wilcox, B. (eds) *A Comprehensive Guide to the Activities Catalogue: An Alternative Curriculum for Youths and Adults with Severe Learning Difficulties,* pxx. Baltimore, MD: Paul H. Brookes Publishing.

O'Brien, J. (1990) *Design For Accomplishment.* Georgia, AL: Responsive Systems Associates.

O'Donnell, L. M. and Livingston, R. L. (1991) 'Active exploration of the environment by young children with low vision: a review of the literature', *Journal of Visual Impairment and Blindness* **85**, 287–91.

Orelove, F. P. and Sobsey, D. (1991) 'Designing transdisciplinary services' in Orelove, F. P. and Sobsey, D. (eds) *Educating Children with Multiple Disabilities: A Transdisciplinary Approach,* 1–31, 2nd edn. Baltimore, MD: Paul H. Brookes Publishing.

Orr, R. (1993) 'Life beyond the room?' *Eye Contact* **6**, 25–6.

Ouvry, C. (1991) 'Access for pupils with profound and multiple learning difficulties' in Ashdown, R., Carpenter, B., Bovair, K. (eds) *The Curriculum Challenge: Access to the National Curriculum for Pupils with Learning Difficulties.* London: Falmer Press.

Pagliano, P. J. (1997a) 'The use of a multisensory environment in education of children with severe multiple disabilities', in Caltabiano, M., Hil, R., Frangos, R. (eds) *Achieving Inclusion: Exploring Issues in Disability,* 73–93. Townsville, Australia: Centre for Social and Welfare Research, James Cook University.

Pagliano, P. J. (1997b) 'The acquisition of communicative competence amongst children with speech and language impairment', in Davies, B and Corson, D. (volume eds) *Oral Discourse and Education,* 157–68. Corson, D. (general ed.) *Encyclopedia of Language and Education,* Dordrecht, The Netherlands: Kluwer Academic Publishers.

Pagliano, P. J. (1998a) 'The multisensory environment: an open minded space', *British Journal of Visual Impairment* **16**, 105–109.

Pagliano, P. J. (1998b) 'Students with vision impairment', in Ashman, A. and Elkins, J. (eds) *Educating Children with Special Needs,* 383–416, 3rd edn. Sydney: Prentice-Hall.

Parker, D., Schembri, A., Johnston, T. (1996) *Technical Signs for Computer Terms: A Sign Reference Book for People in the Computing Field.* North Rocks, NSW: North Rocks Press.

Parmenter, T. R. (1992) 'Quality of life of people with developmental disabilities', *International Review of Research in Mental Retardation* **18**, 247–87.

Pinkney, L. (1997) 'A comparison of the Snoezelen environment and a music relaxation group on the mood and behaviour of patients with senile dementia', *British Journal of Occupational Therapy* **60**(5), 209–12.

Pinkney, L. and Barker, P. (1994) 'Snoezelen – an evaluation of a sensory environment used by people who are elderly and confused', in Hutchinson, R. and Kewin, J. (eds) *Sensations and Disability: Sensory Environments for Leisure, Snoezelen, Education and Therapy*, 172–83. Chesterfield, Derbyshire: Rompa.

Popkewitz, T. S. (1990) 'Whose future? Whose past? Notes on critical theory and methodology', in Guba, E. G. (ed.) *The Paradigm Dialogue*, 46–66. Newbury Park, CA: Sage Publications.

Quon, A. (1998) *Magic of Snoezelen Rooms*, http://www.ability.ns.ca/v5n2/v5n2p3.html

Rawls, J. (1971) *A Theory of Justice*. Cambridge, MA: Harvard University Press.

Reed, L. (1992) 'What's all this about light stimulation?' *Information Exchange*, November, 14–17.

Reed, L. and Addis, C. (1994) 'Learning environments: interactive workboards', *Information Exchange* **41**, 6–8.

Reed, L. and Addis, C. (1996) 'Developing a concept of control', in Bozic, N. and Murdoch, H. (eds) *Learning Through Interaction: Technology and Children with Multiple Disabilities*, 92–105. London: David Fulton Publishers.

Rettig, M. (1994) 'The play of young children with visual impairments: characteristics and interventions', *Journal of Visual Impairment and Blindness* **88**, 410–20.

Rich, P. (1990) *Pamper Your Partner*. London: Hamlyn Publishing.

Rich, P. (1996) *Practical Aromatherapy*. Brookvale, Sydney: The Book Company International.

Rist, R. C. (1975) 'Ethnographic techniques and the urban school', *Urban Education* **10**, 86–108.

Rogers, R. (1997) 'This is tomorrow', The Sunday Review, *Independent on Sunday*, 23 November, 10–16.

ROMPA (1997) *The Complete Resource in Play, Leisure, Therapy and Sport*. Chesterfield, Derbyshire: Rompa.

Ross, M. and Giolas, T. (eds.) (1978) *Auditory Management of Hearing Impaired Children*. Baltimore, MD: University Park Press.

Rotherham, R. (1996) '"Aquatherapy" – a new approach to sensory education', *Eye Contact* **14**, 21–3.

Rubin, K., Fein, G. G., Vandenberg, B. (1983) 'Play' in Mussen, P. H. (ed.) *Handbook of Child Psychology, Vol. 4. Socialization, Personality and Social Development*, 693–774, 4th edn. New York, NY: Wiley.

Sailor, W., Gee, K., Karasoff, P. (1993) 'Full inclusion and school restructuring' in Snell, M. E. (ed.) *Instruction of Students with Severe Disabilities*, 1–30, 4th edn. New York, NY: Merrill.

Sanderson, H. (1995) 'Aromatherapy', in Hogg, J. and Cavet, J. (eds) *Making Leisure Provision for People with Profound Learning and Multiple Disabilities*, 212–26. London: Chapman Hall.

Sanderson, H. and Ruddle, J. (1992) 'Aromatherapy and occupational therapy', *British Journal of Occupational Therapy* **55**(8), 310–14.

Schneekloth, L. H. (1989) 'Play environments for visually impaired children', *Journal of Visual Impairment and Blindness* **83**(4), 196–201.

Scholfield, P. (1994) 'The role of sensation in the management of chronic pain', in Hutchinson, R. and Kewin, J. (eds) *Sensations and Disability: Sensory Environments for Leisure, Snoezelen, Education and Therapy*, 213–28. Chesterfield, Derbyshire: Rompa.

Sebba, J. (1996) 'Foreword', in Rose, R. *et al.* (eds) *Implementing the Whole Curriculum for Pupils with Learning Difficulties*, viii–x. London: David Fulton Publishers.

Sebba, J., Byers, R., Rose, R. (1993) *Redefining the Whole Curriculum for Pupils with Learning Difficulties*. London: David Fulton Publishers.

Shalock, R. (1988) 'Disabled people and the 21st century', in Bartnik, E. A., Lewis, G. M., O'Connor P. (eds) *Technology, Resources and Consumer Outcomes*, 1–10. Perth, Australia: ASSID.

Skellenger, A. C. and Hill, E. W. (1994) 'Effects of a shared teacher–child play intervention on the play skills of three young children who are blind', *Journal of Visual Impairment and Blindness* **88**, 433–45.

Slane, M. (1993) 'Dear editor', *Eye Contact* **7**, 13.

Smith, K. and McAllister, P. (1994) 'Snoezelen – experiences from a day hospital for adults with mental difficulties', in Hutchinson, R. and Kewin, J. (eds) *Sensations and Disability: Sensory Environments for Leisure, Snoezelen, Education and Therapy*, 184–95. Chesterfield, Derbyshire: Rompa.

Solomon, P. *et al.* (1961) *Sensory Deprivation: A Synopsis*. Cambridge, MA: Harvard University Press.

Sparrow, S., Balla, D. A., Cicchetti, D. V. (1984) *Vineland Adaptive Behavior Scales*. Circle Pines, MN: American Guidance Service.

Spradley, J. P. (1980) *Participant Observation*. New York, NY: Holt, Rinehart & Winston.

Stainback, S. and Stainback, W. (1988) *Understanding and Conducting Qualitative Research*. Dubuque, IA: Kendall Hunt.

Starr, K. (1991) 'What is social justice?', *Curriculum Perspectives – Newsletter Edition*, September, 20–24.

Taylor, J. (1995) 'A different voice in occupational therapy', *British Journal of Occupational Therapy* 58(4),170–3.

Taylor, S. and Bogdan, R. (1990) 'Quality of life and the individual's perspective', in Schalock, R. and Begab, M. (eds) *Quality Of Life: Perspectives and Issues*. Washington, DC: American Association on Mental Retardation.

TFH (1997) *Fun and Achievement for people of all Ages with Special Needs* 14. Stourport-on-Severn, Worcs: TFH.

Thompson, S. B. N. and Martin, S. (1994) 'Making sense of multisensory rooms for people with learning disabilities', *British Journal of Occupational Therapy* 57(9), 341–4.

Tröster, H. and Brambring, M. (1994) 'The play behavior and play materials of blind and sighted infants and preschoolers', *Journal of Visual Impairment and Blindness* 88, 421–32.

Ulrich, M. (1991) 'Evaluating evaluation: a 'fictional ' play', in Meyer, L. H., Peck, C. A., Brown, L. (eds) *Critical Issues in the Lives of People with Severe Disabilities*, 93–100. Baltimore, MD: Paul H. Brookes Publishing.

Vitagliano, J. (1988) 'Mother–infant activities: the initial step in language development in the deaf-blind child', in Prickett, H. and Duncan, E. (eds) *Coping with Multi-Handicapped Hearing Impaired: A Practical Approach*, 37–44. Springfield, IL: Charles C. Thomas.

Vygotsky, L. S. (1978) *Mind in Society: The Development of Higher Psychological Processes*. Cambridge, MA: Harvard University Press.

Walls, J. and Dayan, V. S. (1992) 'Adding a sound dimension to the garden, playground or park: sound sculptures', *Information Exchange*, November, 18.

Wang, M. C., Reynolds, M. C., Walberg, H. J. (eds) (1990) *Special Education Research and Practice*. Oxford: Pergamon.

Webber, G. (1995) 'Occupational therapy: a postmodern perspective', *British Journal of Occupational Therapy* 58(10), 439–40.

Westland, G. (1993a) 'Massage as a therapeutic tool, part 1', *British Journal of Occupational Therapy* 56(4), 129–34.

Westland, G. (1993b) 'Massage as a therapeutic tool, part 2', *British Journal of Occupational Therapy* 56(5), 177–80.

White, O. R. (1985) 'The evaluation of severely mentally retarded individuals' in Bricker, B. and Filler, J. (eds) *Severe Mental Retardation: From Theory to Practice*, 161–184. Reston, VA: Council for Exceptional Children.

Whittaker, J. (1992) 'Can anyone help me understand the logic of Snoezelen?' *Community Living*, October, 15.

Willis, S. and Kissane, B. (1997) *Achieving Outcome-Based Education: Premises, Principles and Implications for Curriculum and Assessment*. Perth, Australia: School of Education, Murdoch University.

Winter, R. (1996) 'Some principles and procedures for the conduct of action research', in Zuber-Skerritt , O. (ed.) *New Directions in Action Research*, 13–27. London: Falmer Press.

Wolfensberger, W. (1972) *The Principle of Normalization in Human Services*. Toronto: National Institute on Mental Retardation.

Wolfensberger, W. (1984) 'A reconceptualisation of normalization as social role valorization', *Mental Retardation* 34, 22–7.

Wood, D. (1991) 'Aspects of teaching and learning', in Light, P., Sheldon, S., Woodhead, M. (eds) *Learning to Think*, 97–120. London: Routledge.

Woodill, G. (1994) 'The social semiotics of disability', in Rioux, M. H. and Bach, M. (eds) *Disability is Not Measles: New Research Paradigms in Disability*, 201–26. North York, Ontario: L'Institut Roeher Institute.

Yin, R. K. (1981) *Case Study Research: Design and Methods*. Beverly Hills, CA: Sage Publications.

Index